CW01621837

WHSmith

Revise
Maths

KS3: YEAR 8
Book 1

Age 12–13

Hilary Koll
and Steve Mills

First published in 2007
exclusively for WHSmith by
Hodder Education, an Hachette UK company,
338 Euston Road
London
NW1 3BH

Impression number 10 9 8 7 6 5 4
Year 2011

A CIP record for this book is available from the British Library.

Cover illustration by: Sally Newton Illustrations

Typeset by GreenGate Publishing Services, Tonbridge, Kent

ISBN-13: 978 0 340 94296 3

Printed and bound in Spain

Contents

	How to use this book	4
1	Place value	6
2	Fractions	8
3	Percentages	10
4	Proportion	12
5	Ratio	14
6	Integers	16
7	Factors and multiples	18
8	Powers and roots	20
9	Test 1	22
10	Calculation strategies	24
11	Calculations and problems	26
12	Simplifying expressions	28
13	Equations	30
14	Formulae and substituting	32
15	Sequences	34
16	Straight line graphs	36
17	Test 2	38
18	Area	40
19	Construction	42
20	Co-ordinates	44
21	2-D shape	46
22	Statistics	48
23	Graphs and charts	50
24	Probability	52
25	Test 3	54
	Answers	56
	Checklist	62
	Glossary	64

How to use this book

What this book will do for you and your child

The *Revise Maths* series is designed to help children, aged 11–14, to revise all the Maths topics in the curriculum at Key Stage 3. There are six books in the series, two for each year group, to cover all the key Mathematics topics specified in the Key Stage 3 National Strategy.

The books are designed to be used by children for on-going revision throughout the year. Each double-page spread provides clear information about the nature of the topic and the key aspects that children are expected to master, and provides opportunities for them to practise and test their own understanding. The books contain a progress checklist to allow your child to take an active role in deciding how well he or she understands the topics and to make decisions about how to organise and structure his or her revision.

By working through both books during one year, your child will encounter all the key Mathematics concepts appropriate for that year group.

The Maths curriculum at KS3 and the National Tests

The Key Stage 3 Strategy is designed to make the most of the time between primary school and GCSEs. It provides training for teachers, materials for pupils and advice for everyone involved in making the classroom experience as effective as possible. The Strategy provides a framework for teaching Mathematics in Years 7, 8 and 9, identifying the aspects of Maths to be taught and the expectations for pupils. The main strands of learning at Key Stage 3 are:

- Using and applying Mathematics to solve problems
- Numbers and the number system
- Calculations
- Algebra
- Shape, space and measures
- Handling data.

Children at Key Stage 3 who attend state schools in England sit National Tests (also known as SATs) at the age of 14. Children in Wales may take the same tests at 14. All children may also sit optional tests aged 12 and 13 and many schools have chosen to adopt these tests. The results are used by the school to assess each child's level of knowledge and progress in Maths, English and Science. They also provide guidance for the child's next teacher when he or she is planning the coming year.

The *Revise* series provides opportunities for children to prepare for these tests, by ensuring that they have considered all the Maths topics appropriate for their particular year group. It is important that this is not a last-minute activity, but forms part of the on-going revision work throughout the year. **The children who succeed in Maths are those who evaluate their own understanding of each topic as they encounter it and take steps to impr ove areas of difficulty by further study.** The *Revise* series provides all the necessary information and guidance to assist children in this.

Levels of attainment

Teachers gain information about your child's progress through testing and on-going teacher assessment and you will be informed each year of your child's level of attainment. Each level is a measure that teachers use to check how much your child knows, understands and can do. National expectations are that by the end of Key Stage 1 pupils achieve at least level 2, by the end of Key Stage 2 level 4 and above, by the end of Key Stage 3 level 5 and above.

Stage	Age	Year	National expectations
Foundation	3–4 4–5		
Key Stage 1	5–6 6–7	Year 1 Year 2	Level 2 and above
Key Stage 2	7–8 8–9 9–10 10–11	Year 3 Year 4 Year 5 Year 6	Level 4 and above
Key Stage 3	11–12 12–13 13–14	Year 7 Year 8 Year 9	Level 5 and above
Key Stage 4	14–15 15–16	Year 10 Year 11	Grade C and above

How to use this book

Encourage your child to use and reuse this book alongside his or her school work. Your child should know which Maths topic he or she is covering in school and so can use the *Revise* series to reinforce and develop his or her understanding of the topic. It is not necessary to work through the topics in the order that they are given. Each double-page spread clearly states the facts, skills or concepts that your child should learn and the checklist on pages 62–63 can be used to keep track of which topics have been mastered.

Throughout the book are revision tips which can guide your child towards developing good working practices. These give suggestions for ways to make revision more effective and the learning more long-lasting. Encourage your child to use the checklist at the back of this book to tick off the topics he or she feels happy with. This will help to increase his or her confidence and will point him or her to other topics where revision is needed.

What can parents do to help?

Learning, and especially revision, is best if active. If your child just reads information he or she is unlikely to retain it all. He or she needs to work, memorise and practise on his or her own. The *Revise* series can help your child to do this effectively. Once a child thinks he or she has mastered a topic it can help if you offer to be the pupil! Can he or she teach it to you? If your child can teach you something, he or she really knows and understands it! Explaining something to someone else is one of the best ways of consolidating learning. This approach also shows that you are interested in the topics your child is learning and are acknowledging and celebrating his or her progress.

What next?

Once children have worked through *Revise* Books 1 and 2 for their year group and are confident with all the topics, they can prepare for the National Tests using the *WHS National Tests Practice Papers* books. These contain Practice tests to be taken under exams conditions and can help you to assess the level at which your child is working.

1: Place value

In this unit you will revise:

- powers of 10
- how to multiply integers and decimals by 0.1 and 0.01
- how to divide integers and decimals by 0.1 and 0.01.

Revision shouldn't just happen when you get close to exams. Students who do well in exams are usually those who have worked hard throughout the year. They know which topics they are good at and those which they need more work on. Do you?

What you should know

Our number system is based on groups of 10. In this table you will see what happens when you keep multiplying by 10, starting with the number one.

B	HM	TM	M	HTh	TTh	Th	H	T	U	
									1	one
								1	0	ten
							1	0	0	one hundred
						1	0	0	0	one thousand
					1	0	0	0	0	ten thousand
				1	0	0	0	0	0	one hundred thousand
			1	0	0	0	0	0	0	one million
		1	0	0	0	0	0	0	0	ten million
	1	0	0	0	0	0	0	0	0	one hundred million
1	0	0	0	0	0	0	0	0	0	one billion

Get started

In Maths and Science a shorthand is used to show very large numbers. Powers are used to show how many times a number has been multiplied by 10.

The number one million, 1 000 000, has been made by multiplying by 10 six times in a row. This can be written as 10^6. Notice that one million has six digits, after the first digit, 1, that are all zeros. Look at these examples:

ten thousand = 10 000 = 10^4

one hundred million = 100 000 000 = 10^8

ten = 10 = 10^1

one = 1 = 10^0 (as it has not been multiplied by 10)

1 Fill in the missing words and powers of 10. One has been done for you.

a) one hundred thousand = 100 000 = 10^5

b) ______________________ = 100 = ________

c) ______________________ = 1 000 000 = ________

d) ______________________ = 10 000 000 = ________

e) ______________________ = 1000 = ________

When you keep **dividing** by 10, decimals are used to show numbers less than 1.

Making a number ten times smaller can be written as a division or a multiplication question: $\div 10$ or $\times 0.1$.

Multiplying by 0.1 is the same as dividing by 10. You must move each digit one place to the **right**.

$683 \times 0.1 = 68.3$

H	T	U	.	t
6	8	3	.	
	6	8	.	3

T	U	t	h	th	
1	0 .				ten
	1 .				one
	0 .	1			one tenth
	0 .	0	1		one hundredth
	0 .	0	0	1	one thousandth

Making a number one hundred times smaller can be written as $\div 100$ or $\times 0.01$.

Multiplying by 0.01 is the same as dividing by 100. You must move each digit two places to the **right**.

2 **Multiply** these numbers by 0.1:

a) 34 ________ **b)** 809 ________ **c)** 0.4 ________ **d)** 0.08 ________ **e)** 0.34 ________

3 **Multiply** these numbers by 0.01:

a) 17 ________ **b)** 2853 ________ **c)** 1.3 ________ **d)** 0.68 ________ **e)** 2.75 ________

Similarly, making a number ten times larger can be written as: $\times 10$ or $\div 0.1$ and making it one hundred times larger can be written as $\times 100$ or $\div 0.01$.

Practice

1 Write these numbers using powers of ten:

a) 1000 ________ **b)** 100 000 ________ **c)** 1 ________

d) 10 000 000 ________ **e)** 10 ________

2 **Divide** these numbers by 0.1:

a) 160 ________ **b)** 3840 ________ **c)** 73 ________

d) 0.2 ________ **e)** 105 ________

3 **Divide** these numbers by 0.01:

a) 600 ________ **b)** 7800 ________ **c)** 35 200 ________

d) 407 ________ **e)** 12 ________

4 Answer these questions:

a) 24×10 ________ **b)** $480 \div 0.1$ ________ **c)** 3.5×100 ________

d) $0.92 \div 0.01$ ________ **e)** $1400 \div 100$ ________ **f)** 250×0.01 ________

g) $4850 \div 10$ ________ **h)** 362×0.1 ________

How did I do?

	✔
I can write powers of 10 in different ways.	☐
I can multiply integers and decimals by 0.1 and 0.01.	☐
I can divide integers and decimals by 0.1 and 0.01.	☐

2: Fractions

In this unit you will revise:
- how to order fractions by writing them with a common denominator
- how to use division to convert a fraction to a decimal
- how to order fractions by converting them to decimals.

It can help to make your own revision notes. When you finish this page, write a few lines to help you remember what you have learnt. Keep them somewhere safe to look at again.

What you should know

A **fraction** is part of something that has been split into equal parts.

The bottom number, or **denominator**, shows how many equal parts the whole has been split into.

The top number, or **numerator**, shows how many of those equal parts are being described.

$\frac{3}{5}$ means that a whole has been split into 5 equal parts and that 3 of these parts are being described.

To change a fraction to an equivalent one, multiply or divide the numerator and denominator by the same number, like this:

$$\frac{2}{7} \xrightarrow{\times 4} \frac{8}{28}$$

Fractions, decimals and **percentages** are ways of describing parts of a whole. A decimal such as 0.354 is equivalent to (has the same value as) the fraction $\frac{354}{1000}$ or $\frac{177}{500}$.

Get started

One way to compare and order fractions is to change them so that every fraction has the same denominator. When comparing $\frac{5}{7}$ and $\frac{3}{4}$, change them to **equivalent fractions** with a common denominator, like this:

$$\frac{5}{7} \xrightarrow{\times 4} \frac{20}{28} \qquad \frac{3}{4} \xrightarrow{\times 7} \frac{21}{28}$$

Then it is easy to see that $\frac{21}{28}$ is larger than $\frac{20}{28}$, so $\frac{3}{4}$ is larger than $\frac{5}{7}$.

1 Compare the fractions in each pair, by changing them to equivalent fractions with a common denominator. Tick the larger fraction each time.

a) $\frac{2}{3}$ and $\frac{5}{8}$ **b)** $\frac{3}{5}$ and $\frac{3}{4}$ **c)** $\frac{5}{6}$ and $\frac{7}{8}$ **d)** $\frac{7}{9}$ and $\frac{8}{10}$ **e)** $\frac{4}{7}$ and $\frac{3}{5}$

__________ __________ __________ __________ __________

2 Put these fractions in order from smallest to largest. Change each so that it has the denominator 24.

$\frac{3}{4}$ $\frac{5}{6}$ $\frac{5}{8}$ $\frac{5}{12}$ $\frac{2}{3}$ ________________________________

There is another way of comparing fractions that can be quicker if you have a calculator:

Change all the fractions into equivalent decimals and compare the decimals.

To change a fraction to a decimal, divide the numerator by the denominator. $\frac{5}{8} = 5 \div 8 = 0.625$.

Order these fractions:	$\frac{2}{3}$	$\frac{3}{8}$	$\frac{4}{5}$	$\frac{7}{10}$	$\frac{3}{4}$
Key in	$2 \div 3$	$3 \div 8$	$4 \div 5$	$7 \div 10$	$3 \div 4$
	0.6666...	**0.375**	**0.8**	**0.7**	**0.75**

When comparing decimals, work from left to right starting at the left-hand digit.

The order from smallest to largest is:	0.375	0.666...	0.7	0.75	0.8
	$\frac{3}{8}$	$\frac{2}{3}$	$\frac{7}{10}$	$\frac{3}{4}$	$\frac{4}{5}$

3 Put these fractions in order from smallest to largest. Use a calculator to change the fractions to decimals.

a) $\frac{1}{4}$ $\frac{3}{5}$ $\frac{5}{8}$ $\frac{2}{9}$ $\frac{3}{10}$ ____________________

b) $\frac{4}{9}$ $\frac{5}{6}$ $\frac{2}{5}$ $\frac{7}{8}$ $\frac{2}{3}$ ____________________

If you don't have a calculator you can still use this method, by dividing on paper like this:

$\mathbf{\frac{3}{4}}$ **3 ÷ 4** $4\overline{)3.{}^{3}0{}^{2}0}$ = **0.75**

Practice

1 Put these fractions in order from smallest to largest. Change each to have a common denominator.

a) $\frac{1}{4}$ $\frac{2}{5}$ $\frac{3}{10}$ $\frac{7}{20}$ ____________________

b) $\frac{5}{6}$ $\frac{7}{12}$ $\frac{3}{4}$ $\frac{5}{8}$ $\frac{2}{3}$ ____________________

c) $\frac{5}{9}$ $\frac{5}{6}$ $\frac{3}{4}$ $\frac{11}{18}$ $\frac{4}{9}$ ____________________

2 Order these fractions and decimals, using a calculator:

a) $\frac{3}{4}$ 0.85 $\frac{3}{5}$ 0.7 $\frac{5}{8}$ ____________________

b) $\frac{8}{15}$ 0.48 0.6 $\frac{2}{3}$ $\frac{7}{10}$ ____________________

c) 0.1666... $\frac{5}{12}$ 0.25 $\frac{3}{8}$ $\frac{1}{3}$ ____________________

3 Change each fraction to a decimal by dividing on paper:

a) $\frac{1}{5}$ **b)** $\frac{7}{8}$ **c)** $\frac{5}{9}$

How did I do?

	✔
I can order fractions by writing them with a common denominator.	☐
I can use division to convert a fraction to a decimal.	☐
I can order fractions by converting them to decimals.	☐

3: Percentages

In this unit you will revise:

- how to calculate percentages of numbers and quantities mentally
- how to write one number as a percentage of another without a calculator
- how to write one number as a percentage of another with a calculator.

When writing your own revision notes draw diagrams and pictures to help you remember information. It is sometimes easier to remember a picture than words.

What you should know

Percentages can be used to show parts of a whole. A percentage is a fraction with a denominator of 100, but written in a different way.

36% means $\frac{36}{100}$.

Per cent means out of a hundred. So 36% is read as 'thirty-six per cent' or 'thirty six out of a hundred'.

Here are some ways to calculate percentages mentally:

To find **50%**:	halve the number	To find **10%**:	just divide the number by 10
To find **25%**:	halve the number and halve the answer (or you can just divide by 4)	To find **75%**:	halve the number and halve the answer then add your two answers together
To find **20%**:	divide by 10 and multiply by 2 (double)	To find **30%**:	divide by 10 and multiply by 3
To find **40%**:	divide by 10 and multiply by 4	To find **60%**:	divide by 10 and multiply by 6
To find **70%**:	divide by 10 and multiply by 7	To find **80%**:	divide by 10 and multiply by 8
To find **90%**:	divide by 10 and multiply by 9	To find **5%**:	divide by 10 and then halve the answer
To find **1%**:	just divide the number by 100		

Get started

Many percentages of amounts can be calculated in your head, using some of the strategies listed above.

For example, if you need to find 15% of a number, first find 10% and 5% and add the two answers together. The example below shows how to find 61% of a number:

Find 61% of 120.

To find 60%: divide by 10 and multiply by 6 $120 \div 10 \times 6 = 12 \times 6 = 72$

To find 1%: just divide the number by 100 $120 \div 100 = 1.2$

$72 + 1.2 = \mathbf{73.2}$

1 Answer these percentage questions **without** a calculator:

a) 11% of £110 ________ **b)** 15% of 48 m ________ **c)** 35% of £60 ________

d) 21% of 300 g ________ **e)** 51% of 210 cm ________ **f)** 26% of 80 m ________

g) 76% of 40 cm ________ **h)** 95% of 120 kg ________

To write a number, such as a test score, as a percentage of another, make a fraction and then change the fraction to a percentage. Remember that a percentage is a fraction with a denominator of 100.

"I scored 42 out of 50."

$$\frac{42}{50} \xrightarrow{\times 2} \frac{84}{100} = 84\%$$

"I scored 6 out of 10."

$$\frac{6}{10} \xrightarrow{\times 10} \frac{60}{100} = 60\%$$

"I scored 425 out of 500."

$$\frac{425}{500} \xrightarrow{\div 5} \frac{85}{100} = 85\%$$

2 Write each score as a percentage:

a) 13 out of 20 ________ **b)** 8 out of 25 ________ **c)** 4 out of 5 ________

d) 6 out of 10 ________ **e)** 14 out of 50 ________ **f)** 225 out of 500 ________

g) 18 out of 25 ________ **h)** 180 out of 200 ________

If the denominator of the fraction cannot be multiplied or divided easily to make 100, divide the numerator by the denominator on a calculator and multiply by 100.

I scored 42 out of 47. $\rightarrow 42 \div 47 \times 100 = 89.3617$ Round the answer $\rightarrow$ 89.4%

Practice

1 Fill in the missing amounts in this diagram, finding different percentages of £240. Do **not** use a calculator. One has been done for you.

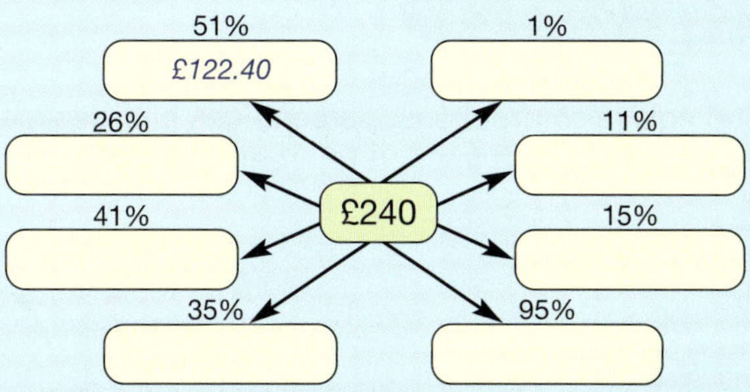

2 Andy, Mandy and Sandy took different Maths tests.

Andy scored 8 out of 10, Mandy scored 21 out of 25, Sandy scored 210 out of 300.

Write these scores as percentages (without a calculator) and tick the person with the highest percentage:

Andy ________% Mandy ________% Sandy ________%

3 On a mountain, the wind speed was recorded as gale force on 292 days out of 365 last year. What percentage is this? You may use a calculator.

________%

4 In a phone-in vote, approximately 13 million out of 19 million voted for the winner. About what percentage is this? You may use a calculator.

________%

How did I do?

	✔
I can calculate percentages of numbers and quantities mentally.	☐
I can write one number as a percentage of another without a calculator.	☐
I can write one number as a percentage of another with a calculator.	☐

4: Proportion

In this unit you will revise:

- the equivalence of percentages, fractions and decimals
- how to use fractions, decimals and percentages to compare proportions.

When you are revising, take regular breaks. Doing some exercises can help you to feel more alert and will help you to concentrate better.

What you should know

Proportion has several meanings in Maths. Someone can ask 'What proportion of these sweets are red?' Proportion, here, means 'part of the whole set' and could be answered using a **fraction**, a **decimal** or a **percentage**. The answer could be 'A quarter ($\frac{1}{4}$) of them are red' or '0.25 are red' or '25% are red'.

Fractions, decimals and percentages are all used to describe parts of a whole.

It is important to know fractions, decimals and percentages with the same values. This number line shows how some of them are related.

0	10%	20%	30%	40%	50%	60%	70%	80%	90%	100%
0	0.1	0.2	0.3	0.4	0.5	0.6	0.7	0.8	0.9	1
0	$\frac{1}{10}$	$\frac{1}{5}$	$\frac{3}{10}$	$\frac{2}{5}$	$\frac{1}{2}$	$\frac{3}{5}$	$\frac{7}{10}$	$\frac{4}{5}$	$\frac{9}{10}$	1

Get started

This diagram shows how to find equivalent fractions, percentages and decimals. Move clockwise around the diagram, changing from a percentage to a fraction to a decimal and so on. Use a calculator.

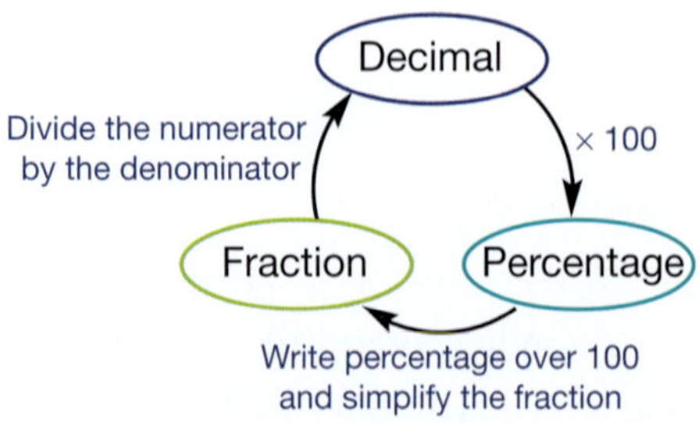

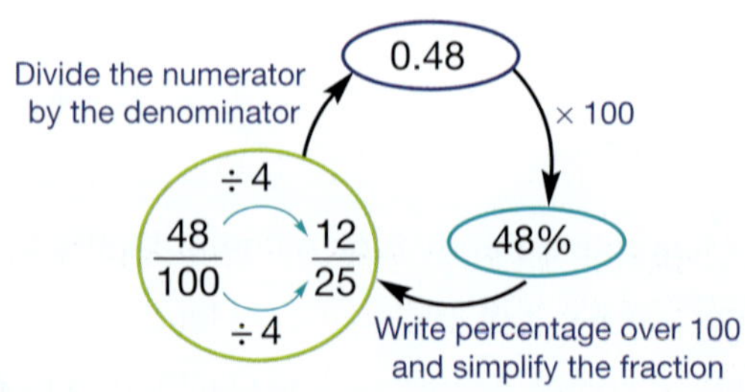

1 Write the fraction, decimal and percentage equivalents to complete these tables. Give fractions in their simplest form.

a)

F	D	P
$\frac{1}{10}$		
$\frac{3}{4}$		
$\frac{27}{100}$		

b)

D	P	F
0.01		
0.4		
0.81		

c)

P	F	D
27%		
5%		
20%		

This clothing label shows proportions of material that add up to 1 whole or 100%:

- To find the **percentage** of the material that is cotton, change all the proportions to percentages, find their total and subtract it from 100%.
- To find the **fraction** of the material that is cotton, change all the proportions to fractions with the same denominator (such as 100), find the total and subtract it from 1.

20% nylon
$\frac{1}{10}$ lycra
$\frac{2}{5}$ wool
10% polyester
______ cotton

20% nylon	$\frac{2}{10}$ nylon
10% lycra	$\frac{1}{10}$ lycra
40% wool	$\frac{4}{10}$ wool
10% polyester	$\frac{1}{10}$ polyester
80% $\quad 100 - 80 = 20$	$\frac{8}{10} \quad 1 - \frac{8}{10} = \frac{2}{10} = \frac{1}{5}$
20% cotton	$\frac{1}{5}$ cotton

Practice

1 **a)** What fraction is silk?

35% nylon
$\frac{1}{100}$ lycra
$\frac{8}{50}$ viscose
9% nylon
? silk

__________ silk

b) What percentage is viscose?

$\frac{3}{10}$ polyester
12% nylon
$\frac{2}{5}$ lycra
$\frac{1}{10}$ silk
? viscose

__________ viscose

c) What fraction is elastane?

$\frac{1}{25}$ lycra
8% nylon
$\frac{7}{50}$ polyester
$\frac{1}{10}$ cotton
? elastane

__________ elastane

d) What percentage is wool?

12% elastane
$\frac{1}{10}$ polyester
$\frac{7}{20}$ lycra
$\frac{3}{25}$ silk
? wool

__________ wool

2 What proportion of each shape is shaded? Give each answer as a fraction in its simplest form, as a decimal, and as a percentage.

a) 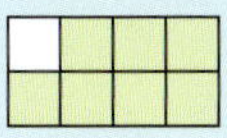 ______

______ ______

b) 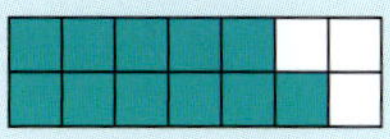 ______

______ ______

c) 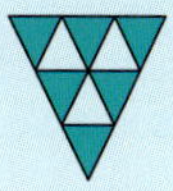 ______

______ ______

3 At a concert the proportion of the whole crowd that is male is 17%. What proportion of the crowd is female? Give your answer as a decimal, as a percentage and as a fraction.

______ ______ ______

How did I do?

	✔
I understand that percentages, fractions and decimals can be equivalent.	☐
I can change between fractions, decimals and percentages.	☐
I can use fractions, decimals and percentages to compare proportions.	☐

5: Ratio

In this unit you will revise:

- how to reduce a ratio to its simplest form
- how to reduce a ratio in different units to its simplest form
- how to divide a quantity into two or more parts in a given ratio.

When you are revising, if you don't understand something immediately, don't panic. Read it through several times and ask someone for help. Perhaps a teacher or an older brother or sister can help you.

What you should know

Ratio is the relationship between two or more numbers or quantities. It compares 'part with part'.

Look at this rod: 

If we compare the *red parts* with the *white parts* we can say '3 red squares for every 2 white squares' so the **ratio** of red to white is 3 to 2, written **3 : 2**.

Get started

To **simplify** a ratio divide the parts of the ratio by the same number.

Write the ratio 24 : 16 in its simplest form:

24 : 16
÷ 2 → 12 : 8 ← ÷ 2
÷ 2 → 6 : 4 ← ÷ 2
÷ 2 → 3 : 2 ← ÷ 2

24 : 16
÷ 8 → 3 : 2 ← ÷ 8

So 24 : 16 is simplified and shown to be **equivalent** to 3 : 2. When simplifying, try to divide by the largest number you can. When you cannot divide any more to get whole numbers, the ratio is said to be in its **simplest form**.

1 Write each ratio in its **simplest form.**

a) 6 : 9 ________ **b)** 10 : 24 ________ **c)** 32 : 8 ________ **d)** 15 : 25 ________

e) 3 : 15 ________ **f)** 12 : 24 ________ **g)** 24 : 16 ________ **h)** 18 : 54 ________

Sometimes a ratio has numbers in different units of measurement:

This line is split into two parts: 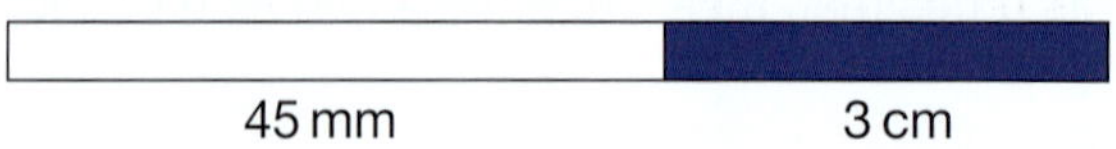

The ratio of white to blue is: 45 mm : 3 cm

To write this ratio in its simplest form you must change the measurements so that both are in the same unit, the smaller unit, and then divide to write it in its simplest form.

45 mm : 3 cm
45 mm : 30 mm
÷ 15 → 3 : 2 ← ÷ 15

The ratio of white to blue in the line is 3 : 2, in its simplest form.

2 Write each ratio in its **simplest form.**

a) 2 m : 50 cm ________ **b)** 450 g : 5 kg ________ **c)** 5 mm : 7.5 cm ________

d) 1500 ml : 2 litres ________ **e)** 3.5 cm : 28 mm ________ **f)** 650 cm : 5 m ________

To divide an amount into two or more parts in a given ratio, first find out how many parts in the ratio there are altogether. Then divide the total number or amount by the number of parts altogether to find how much one part is worth.

Mr Collyer gives his three daughters, Lucy, Emily and Alice, some money in the ratio 5 : 3 : 4. How much will they each get if Mr Collyer gives them a total of £48?

The ratio is 5 : 3 : 4.

There are 5 + 3 + 4 = 12 parts altogether.

Divide £48 by 12 to find out how much one part is worth. 48 ÷ 12 = 4.

This means that each part is worth £4.

Lucy gets 5 parts, so multiply 5 by £4. She gets £20.

Emily gets 3 parts, so multiply 3 by £4. She gets £12.

Alice gets 4 parts, so multiply 4 by £4. She gets £16.

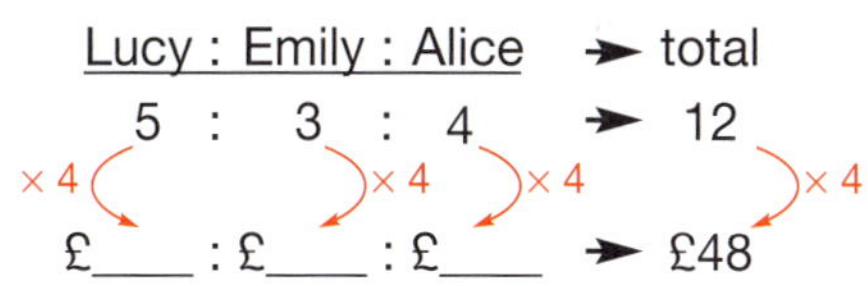

Check that the total is £48. £20 + £12 + £16 = £48 ✔

Practice

1 Write each ratio in its **simplest form**.

a) 2.5 m : 25 cm ________ **b)** 500 g : 4 kg ________ **c)** 42 mm : 7 cm ________

2 Answer these ratio questions.

a) At a party of 63 people the ratio of males to females was 5 : 2. How many were males and how many were females?

Males ________ Females ________

b) Ali, Baz and Colin win £80 and agree to share the money in the ratio 1 : 2 : 5. How much does each get?

Ali ________ Baz ________ Colin ________

c) Deepa, Ella and Fee win £160 and agree to share the money in the ratio 1 : 4 : 5. How much does each get?

Deepa ________ Ella ________ Fee ________

How did I do?

	✔
I can reduce a ratio to its simplest form.	☐
I can reduce a ratio in different units to its simplest form.	☐
I can divide a quantity into two or more parts in a given ratio.	☐

6: Integers

In this unit you will revise:

- adding and subtracting integers
- multiplying and dividing integers.

When revising, use the checklist at the back of this book to tick off the topics you feel happy with. This will help to increase your confidence and will point you to other topics you need to revise.

What you should know

Integers are the set of numbers made up of **positive** and **negative** whole **numbers** and zero. These are all integers: 5, 125, 4, –6, 0, –27, 36, –100.

Here some are shown on a number line.

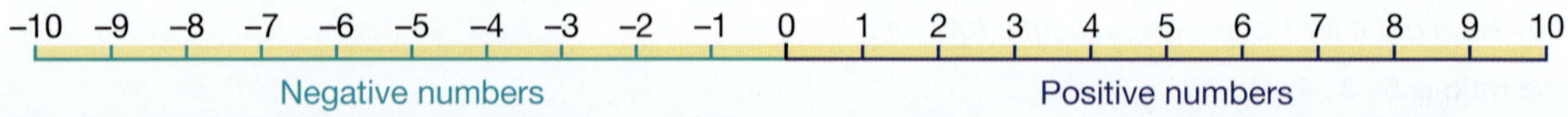

On this line, the numbers get smaller as you move to the left and get larger as you move to the right.

Get started

When **adding** numbers, count along the number line, moving towards the **right**:

$-10 + 2 =$ (answer is –8)

Point to –10 on the line → –10; move to the right → +; 2 places → 2

When **subtracting** numbers, count along the number line, moving towards the **left**:

$-3 - 5 =$ (answer is –8)

Point to –3 on the line → –3; move to the left → –; 5 places → 5

1 Answer these questions, moving along the number line:

a) $-5 + 8 =$ ________ **b)** $-3 + 6 =$ ________ **c)** $-5 + 9 =$ ________

d) $-1 + 7 =$ ________ **e)** $-4 + 8 =$ ________ **f)** $-6 - 2 =$ ________

g) $4 - 8 =$ ________ **h)** $-2 - 8 =$ ________

i) $0 - 5 =$ ________ **j)** $-6 - 3 =$ ________

Sometimes, when you are adding and subtracting, two signs appear next to each other, like these:

$1 - -3 =$ (subtraction sign; the number –3)

$-3 + -4 =$ (addition sign; the number –4)

If this happens, there are some rules you can follow to make it easier:

– – think of as a +
+ – think of as a –

So you can rewrite the questions to make them easier to answer, like this:

$1 - -3 =$
$1 + 3 = 4$

$-3 + -4 =$
$-3 - 4 = -7$

2 Change each question to make it easier to answer and then answer it. One has been done for you.

a) 1 – –4 = **1 + 4 = 5**

b) –5 – –8 = ______

c) –4 + –7 = ______

d) 6 + –4 = ______

e) 8 – –8 = ______

f) –3 + –3 = ______

When **multiplying** and **dividing** integers, treat them as if they are **positive numbers** first and write down the answer. Then look at whether the numbers in the question are both positive or both negative or one of each. Use the information below to help you decide what sign the answer should have:

positive × positive = positive	3 × 5 = 15
positive ÷ positive = positive	15 ÷ 5 = 3
positive × negative = negative	3 × –5 = –15
positive ÷ negative = negative	15 ÷ –5 = –3
negative × positive = negative	–3 × 5 = –15
negative ÷ positive = negative	–15 ÷ 5 = –3
negative × negative = positive	–3 × –5 = 15
negative ÷ negative = positive	–15 ÷ –5 = 3

Practice

1 Answer these addition and subtraction questions:

a) –3 – 1 = ______ **b)** –5 – –9 = ______ **c)** 0 + –4 = ______

d) –4 + 14 = ______ **e)** –7 + 10 = ______ **f)** 6 – –9 = ______

g) –1 + –4 = ______ **h)** –6 – –2 = ______

2 Answer these multiplication and division questions:

a) –1 × –10 = ______ **b)** –5 × 9 = ______ **c)** –30 ÷ 10 = ______

d) –35 ÷ –5 = ______ **e)** 4 × –10 = ______ **f)** –6 × –8 = ______

g) –36 ÷ –4 = ______ **h)** 32 ÷ –8 = ______ **i)** –5 × –2 = ______

j) 6 × –4 = ______ **k)** –27 ÷ –9 = ______ **l)** –16 ÷ 4 = ______

Now use a calculator to check your answers.

3 Here are five number cards.

Which of the cards can be used to make these statements correct? [–18] [–4] [6] [–6] [–3]

Fill in the numbers.

a) ☐ + ☐ = –10 **b)** ☐ – ☐ = 3 **c)** ☐ × ☐ = –24 **d)** ☐ ÷ ☐ = 3

How did I do?

	✔
I can add and subtract integers.	☐
I can multiply and divide integers.	☐

7: Factors and multiples

In this unit you will revise:

- what factors and multiples are and how to find factors and multiples of numbers
- how to find common factors and to find the highest common factor
- how to find common multiples and to find the lowest common multiple.

What you should know

Factors are whole numbers that divide exactly into another number without a remainder. Every whole number has the factor 1 and itself. The factors of 12 are **1**, **2**, **3**, **4**, **6** and **12** as they are the only whole numbers that divide exactly into 12 without a remainder.

Learn these simple tests to see what factors a number has:

- If a number is even, it has the factor **2**.
- If the digits add up to a multiple of 3, it has the factor **3**.
- If, when halved, the answer is even, it has the factor **4**.
- If a number ends in 0 or 5, it has the factor **5**.
- If it's even and if the digits add up to a multiple of 3, it has the factor **6**.
- If, when halved and halved again, the answer is even, it has the factor **8**.
- If the digits add up to a multiple of 9, it has the factor **9**.
- If a number ends in 0, it has the factor **10**.

To see whether 7 is a factor, use a calculator to divide the number by 7. If the answer is a whole number then 7 is a factor.

A **multiple** is a number that is in a times table or beyond. Multiples of 5 are 5, 10, 15, 20, 25, 30, ... and carry on, such as 85, 115, 500. The answer to a multiplication question is a multiple of both the numbers multiplied, for example, $6 \times 7 = 42$, so 42 is a **multiple** of 6 and 7.

Get started

A number is a **common factor** if it divides into more than one number.

The factors of **24** are **1**, **2**, **3**, **4**, **6**, **8**, **12** and **24**. The factors of **18** are **1**, **2**, **3**, **6**, **9** and **18**.

So the **common factors** of **24** and **18** are **1**, **2**, **3** and **6** (the factors in both lists).

Notice that the **highest common factor** of 24 and 18 is the factor **6**.

1 Find the factors of the two numbers given and write down the common factors:

a) 12 and 24 ____________ **b)** 45 and 27 ____________

c) 28 and 32 ____________ **d)** 18 and 30 ____________

e) 24 and 40 ____________ **f)** 30 and 36 ____________

2 For each pair above write the highest common factor.

a) ________ **b)** ________ **c)** ________ **d)** ________

e) ________ **f)** ________

A number is a **common multiple** if it is a multiple of more than one number.

Some multiples of 3:

3	6	9	12	15	18	21	24	27	30

Some multiples of 4:

4	8	12	16	20	24	28	32

As 12 and 24 appear in both lists, **12** and **24** are **common multiples** of **3** and **4**.

Notice that **12** is the **lowest common multiple** of **3** and **4** as it is the lowest number that appears in both lists.

3 Find some multiples of the two numbers given and write down three common multiples:

a) 3 and 5 ________ ________ ________

b) 4 and 6 ________ ________ ________

c) 7 and 4 ________ ________ ________

d) 9 and 3 ________ ________ ________

e) 5 and 7 ________ ________ ________

f) 6 and 8 ________ ________ ________

4 For each pair above write the lowest common multiple.

a) ________

b) ________

c) ________

d) ________

e) ________

f) ________

Practice

1 James picks two number cards and finds the highest common factor of the two numbers.

72	35	42	80	54

Which two numbers has he chosen if the highest common factor is:

a) 8? _______ _______

b) 6 (there are 2 possible answers)? _______ _______

c) 7? _______ _______

d) 5? _______ _______

e) 2 (there are 2 possible answers)? _______ _______

f) 18? _______ _______

2 Find the **lowest common multiple** of:

a) 11 and 6 _______

b) 10 and 8 _______

c) 12 and 4 _______

d) 5 and 12 _______

e) 15 and 4 _______

How did I do?

	✔
I know what a factor is and can find factors of numbers.	☐
I know what a multiple is and can find multiples of numbers.	☐
I can find common factors and say which is the highest common factor.	☐
I can find common multiples and say which is the lowest common multiple.	☐

8: Powers and roots

In this unit you will revise:

- squares and cubes including how to write them using powers
- square roots and cube roots.

Revise in small bursts. Don't spend more than 30–45 minutes working without a break.

What you should know

These numbers are called **square numbers**:

1 4 9 16 25 36 49 64 81 100 121 144 ...

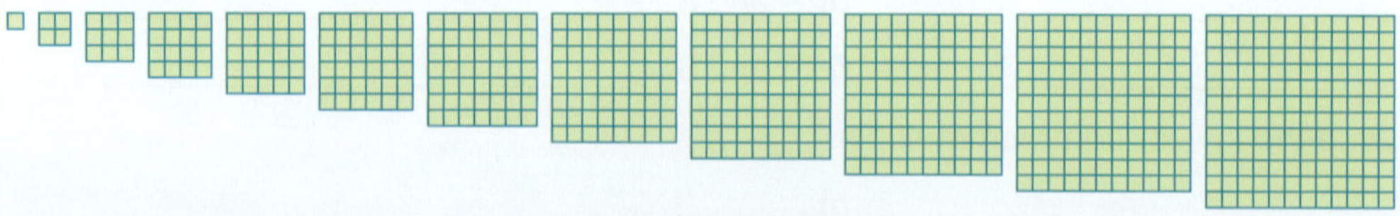

If we multiply a whole number by itself the answer is a square number.

Square numbers are created by '**squaring**' a number:

1^2 (1 squared) $= 1 \times 1 =$ **1**

2^2 (2 squared) $= 2 \times 2 =$ **4**

3^2 (3 squared) $= 3 \times 3 =$ **9**

4^2 (4 squared) $= 4 \times 4 =$ **16**

Finding the **square root** is the opposite of squaring. The number being multiplied by itself is found. Square roots are written using the $\sqrt{}$ sign. $\sqrt{16}$ means 'What number is multiplied by itself to make 16?'. The answer is 4, because $4 \times 4 = 16$.

$\sqrt{\mathbf{1}}$ (the square root of 1) $= 1$

$\sqrt{\mathbf{4}}$ (the square root of 4) $= 2$

$\sqrt{\mathbf{9}}$ (the square root of 9) $= 3$

$\sqrt{\mathbf{16}}$ (the square root of 16) $= 4$

Get started

Both positive and negative numbers can be squared. Watch what happens when a positive or negative number is squared (multiplied by itself):

$4^2 = 4 \times 4 = 16$

$(-4)^2 = -4 \times -4 = 16$

When two **negative numbers** are multiplied the answer is positive (see page 17).

When *any* negative number is squared the answer will be positive. Notice also that you get the same answer for both questions above. This means that there are two answers to the question 'What is the square root of 16?'. There are two different numbers that can be multiplied by themselves to make 16: 4 and –4. To show the two answers the ± sign is used:

$\sqrt{16} = \pm 4$

1 Write the value, remembering to use the ± sign for square root questions.

a) $(-7)^2$ ________ **b)** $\sqrt{25}$ ________ **c)** $(-9)^2$ ________ **d)** $\sqrt{49}$ ________ **e)** 10^2 ________

f) $(-5)^2$ ________ **g)** $\sqrt{4}$ ________ **h)** 6^2 ________ **i)** $\sqrt{9}$ ________ **j)** $(-12)^2$ ________

Here are the first five cubic numbers: **1 8 27 64 125 ...**

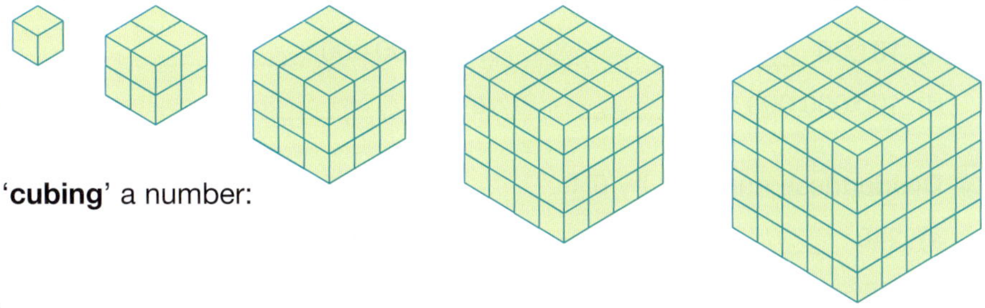

If we multiply three numbers that are the same together the answer is a cubic number.

Cubic numbers are created by '**cubing**' a number:

1^3 (1 cubed) $= 1 \times 1 \times 1 =$ **1**
2^3 (2 cubed) $= 2 \times 2 \times 2 =$ **8**
3^3 (3 cubed) $= 3 \times 3 \times 3 =$ **27**
4^3 (4 cubed) $= 4 \times 4 \times 4 =$ **64**

Finding the **cube root** is the opposite of cubing. Cube roots are written using the $\sqrt[3]{\ }$ sign.

$\sqrt[3]{27} = 3$, because $3 \times 3 \times 3 = 27$.

$\sqrt[3]{\mathbf{1}}$ (the cube root of 1) = 1
$\sqrt[3]{\mathbf{8}}$ (the cube root of 8) = 2
$\sqrt[3]{\mathbf{27}}$ (the cube root of 27) = 3
$\sqrt[3]{\mathbf{64}}$ (the cube root of 64) = 4

2 Write the value of:

a) 5^3 ________ **b)** $\sqrt[3]{64}$ ________ **c)** $\sqrt[3]{8}$ ________ **d)** 10^3 ________ **e)** $\sqrt[3]{1}$ ________

Practice

1 Use a calculator to find the value of:

a) $(-32)^2$ ________ **b)** $\sqrt{2916}$ ________ **c)** 48^2 ________ **d)** $\sqrt{8464}$ ________

e) $(-13)^2$ ________ **f)** 7^3 ________ **g)** $\sqrt[3]{512}$ ________ **h)** $\sqrt[3]{216}$ ________

i) 9^3 ________ **j)** 11^3 ________

2 Use your calculator to help you mark Sandeep's work. If there is a mistake, correct it.

a) $\sqrt{324} = 18$ ________ **b)** $45^2 = 2225$ ________ **c)** $\sqrt[3]{4913} = 17$ ________

d) $64^3 = 4$ ________ **e)** $(0.1)^2 = 0.1$ ________ **f)** $\sqrt{71\,824} = 268$ ________

g) $\sqrt[3]{300.763} = 6.7$ ________ **h)** $65^3 = 274\,625$ ________ **i)** $(13.7)^3 = 2571.353$ ________

3 Answer these mental Maths test questions:

a) Write the value of seven squared. ________ **b)** What is the square root of sixteen? ________

c) What is the difference in value between eight squared and four cubed? ________

d) Look at these **expressions**. Tick which is equivalent to *n* times *n*.

n^3 $\sqrt{n}$ n^2 $\sqrt[3]{n}$

e) Tick which of these is the best estimate of the square root of 47.

6.1 8.2 6.9 5.5 23.5

How did I do?

	✔
I know how to write squares and cubes using powers.	☐
I can find squares and cubes of numbers with and without a calculator.	☐
I can find square roots and cube roots of numbers.	☐

9: Test 1

1. Write these numbers using powers of ten:

a) 10 000 __________ b) 1 000 000 __________ c) 10 __________

d) 100 000 000 __________ e) 1 __________

2. **Divide** these numbers by 0.1:

a) 240 __________ b) 6430 __________ c) 69 __________

d) 0.4 __________ e) 306 __________

3. **Divide** these numbers by 0.01:

a) 700 __________ b) 4400 __________ c) 26 200 __________

d) 503 __________ e) 16 __________

4. Answer these questions:

a) 37×10 __________ b) $470 \div 0.1$ __________ c) 2.8×100 __________

d) $0.69 \div 0.01$ __________ e) $2700 \div 100$ __________ f) 290×0.01 __________

g) $1550 \div 10$ __________ h) 427×0.1 __________

5. Put these fractions in order from smallest to largest. Change each to have a common denominator.

a) $\frac{3}{5}$ $\frac{9}{20}$ $\frac{3}{4}$ $\frac{7}{10}$ ______________________________

b) $\frac{4}{6}$ $\frac{5}{12}$ $\frac{3}{8}$ $\frac{2}{3}$ ______________________________

6. Order these fractions and decimals, using a calculator:

a) $\frac{11}{12}$ 0.48 0.75 $\frac{2}{3}$ $\frac{7}{10}$ ______________________________

b) $\frac{5}{6}$ $\frac{9}{12}$ 0.25 $\frac{3}{8}$ 0.3333 ______________________________

7. Andy, Mandy and Sandy took different Maths tests.

Andy scored 7 out of 10, Mandy scored 19 out of 25, and Sandy scored 195 out of 300.

Write these scores as percentages (without a calculator) and tick the person with the highest percentage.

Andy __________% Mandy __________% Sandy __________%

8. Write the fraction, decimal and percentage equivalents to complete these tables. Give fractions in their simplest form.

a)

F	D	P
$\frac{7}{10}$		
$\frac{2}{5}$		
$\frac{63}{100}$		

b)

D	P	F
0.07		
0.3		
0.17		

c)

P	F	D
33%		
2%		
40%		

9 What proportion of each shape is shaded? Give each answer as a fraction, as a decimal and as a percentage.

a) 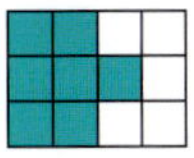 ________ ________ ________

b) 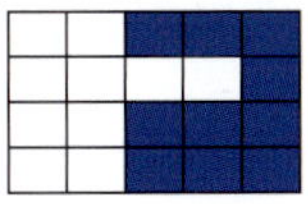 ________ ________ ________

c) 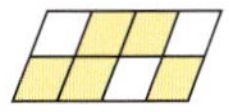 ________ ________ ________

10 Write each ratio in its **simplest form**.

a) 3.5 m : 35 cm ________ b) 600 g : 6 kg ________ c) 24 mm : 8 cm ________

11 Answer these ratio questions:

a) At a party of 35 people the ratio of males to females was 5 : 2. How many were males and how many were females?

Males ________ Females ________

b) Ali, Baz and Colin win £800 and agree to share the money in the ratio 2 : 3 : 5. How much does each get?

Ali ________ Baz ________ Colin ________

c) Deepa, Ella and Fee win £48 and agree to share the money in the ratio 1 : 4 : 7. How much does each get?

Deepa ________ Ella ________ Fee ________

12 Answer these addition and subtraction questions.

a) $-3 - 6 =$ ________ b) $-5 - -11 =$ ________ c) $0 + -8 =$ ________

d) $-9 + 14 =$ ________ e) $-15 + 10 =$ ________ f) $3 - -9 =$ ________

g) $-8 + -4 =$ ________ h) $-10 - -11 =$ ________

13 Answer these multiplication and division questions:

a) $-1 \times -8 =$ ________ b) $-4 \times 9 =$ ________ c) $-30 \div 3 =$ ________

d) $-45 \div -5 =$ ________ e) $6 \times -10 =$ ________ f) $-4 \times -8 =$ ________

g) $-28 \div -4 =$ ________ h) $64 \div -8 =$ ________ i) $-6 \times -2 =$ ________

j) $9 \times -3 =$ ________ k) $-54 \div -9 =$ ________ l) $-32 \div 4 =$ ________

14 Find the **highest common factor** of:

a) 40 and 30 ________ b) 28 and 24 ________ c) 36 and 48 ________

d) 21 and 35 ________ e) 18 and 30 ________

15 Find the **lowest common multiple** of:

a) 11 and 7 ________ b) 4 and 8 ________ c) 12 and 3 ________

d) 8 and 12 ________ e) 15 and 6 ________

16 Use a calculator to find the value of:

a) $(-27)^2$ ________ b) $\sqrt{225}$ ________ c) 35^2 ________ d) $\sqrt{441}$ ________

e) $(-11)^2$ ________ f) 6^3 ________ g) $\sqrt[3]{1000}$ ________ h) $\sqrt[3]{2744}$ ________

i) 8^3 ________ j) 24^3 ________

10: Calculation strategies

In this unit you will revise:

- adding, subtracting, multiplying and dividing using mental methods
- the order of operations, including brackets.

In a written test, always show your working as, even if you make a mistake, you can sometimes get marks for your working out.

What you should know

There are four main **operations** in Maths: adding, subtracting, multiplying and dividing. Some questions involve more than one '**operation**'. Mathematicians have agreed on an order that you must do calculations, otherwise everyone would get different answers, like this:

$\mathbf{4 + 3 \times 5 - 1}$ =	If working from left to right you would get the answer 34.
$\mathbf{4 + 3 \times 5 - 1}$ =	If doing the multiplication part first the answer would be 18.
$\mathbf{4 + 3 \times 5 - 1}$ =	If doing the subtraction and addition parts first the answer could be 28.

To make sure no one gets confused, this is the order that has been agreed:

Do anything in **brackets** first	**Brackets**
Next do **other** things such as squares, roots and powers	**Other**
Then **divide** and **multiply** next	**Divide**
	Multiply
Finally **add** and **subtract**	**Add**
	Subtract

The letters of the word **BODMAS** can help us to remember the order of the operations. So the correct answer to $\mathbf{4 + 3 \times 5 - 1}$ is **18**, because the multiplying must be done before the adding and subtracting.

Sometimes people call the word **BIDMAS** where the letter I stands for Index or Indices, which are powers.

Get started

When a calculation has a division line, write brackets around what is above and below the line. Work them out before you divide.

Like this: $\frac{4+8}{8-2} = \frac{(4+8)}{(8-2)} = \frac{12}{6} = 2$

1 Work out the correct answers for these questions. One has been done for you.

a) $\frac{11+13}{4 \times 2} = \mathbf{\frac{(11+13)}{(4 \times 2)} = \frac{24}{8} = 3}$

b) $\frac{8+12}{4+6}$ = ____________

c) $\frac{22-10}{2 \times 3}$ = ____________

d) $\frac{4 \times 5}{10 \div 2}$ = ____________

e) $\frac{5+11}{2 \times 2}$ = ____________

f) $\frac{15-7}{12 \div 3}$ = ____________

g) $\frac{3 \times 9}{21-18}$ = ____________

h) $\frac{28 \div 7}{72 \div 9}$ = ____________

The **O** in **BODMAS** stands for **Other** operations such as using powers and roots.

When a calculation involves squares, cubes or roots, remember to work them out before division, multiplication, addition and subtraction.

If y is 5, then the value of $2y^2$ is found by first **squaring** 5 and then multiplying by 2, not the other way around.

$2y^2 = 2 \times 25 = 50$

2 If $b = 4$ find the values of:

a) $2b^2$ ________ **b)** $3b^2$ ________ **c)** $5b^2 - 2$ ________

d) $\frac{\sqrt{b}}{2}$ ________ **e)** $\frac{3 \times \sqrt{b}}{6}$ ________ **f)** $\frac{b^2}{\sqrt{b}}$ ________

g) $10 + b^2$ ________ **h)** $b + \sqrt{b} + b^2 \times 2$ ________ **i)** $1 + \frac{b^2}{4}$ ________

Practice

1 Work out the correct answers for these questions. Remember to use the order of **BODMAS**.

a) $\frac{34 + 76}{64 - 53}$ ________ **b)** $\frac{18 + 6}{3 \times 4}$ ________ **c)** $\frac{57 - 22}{52 + 18}$ ________

d) $\frac{\sqrt{25} + 95}{4 \times 5}$ ________ **e)** $\frac{(2 + 3)^2}{(13 - 8)^2}$ ________ **f)** $\frac{\sqrt{16} + 2^3}{4 \times \sqrt{4}}$ ________

2 Tick the expressions below that have a value of 12.

$(1 - 3)^2 \times 3$	$\sqrt{(2^2 + 5)} \times 4$	$96 \div 4 \div 2$
$\frac{(3 \times 2)^2}{\sqrt{(10 - 1)}}$	$\sqrt{((6 + 3) \times 4^2)}$	$\frac{5^2 - 1}{2^2 - 2}$

3 Tick which of these expressions have the value of 100.

a) $0 + 123 - 45 + 67 + 89 =$

b) $0 + 123 - (4 + 5) - (6 + 7) + 8 - 9 =$

c) $(0 + 1) \times (2 + 3) \times 4 + 5 - (6 + 7) + 89 =$

d) $0 + 1 + 2 + 3 - (4 \times 5) + (6 \times 7) + (8 \times 9) =$

e) $0 + (1 \times 234) - (56 + 78) + 9 =$

f) $0 - (1 \times 2) - (3 + 4) - 5 + (6 \times 7) + (8 \times 9) =$

How did I do?

	✔
I can add, subtract, multiply and divide using mental methods.	☐
I know the order that calculations should be carried out (BODMAS).	☐

11: Calculations and problems

In this unit you will revise:

- adding, subtracting, multiplying and dividing decimals using written methods
- how to check a result by working backwards
- how to solve word problems.

When solving a problem, always circle or underline the key numbers. Before calculating, make an approximation by rounding the numbers. Show your working and always remember to check your final answer.

What you should know

Adding, subtracting, multiplying and dividing decimals on paper is similar to calculating with whole numbers. When adding and subtracting decimals using a written method, always make sure that you line up the **decimal points**. Then just add or subtract in the normal way:

```
  T U . t          U . t h          T U . t h
  6 6 . 5          7 . ³4¹3         1 6 . 5
+ 2 3 . 8        - 0 . 2 8      +    2 . 3 8
 ₁9₁0 . 3          7 . 1 5        1 8 . 8 8
```

Get started

When multiplying and dividing decimals on paper, make an approximation first and write it down. Then just multiply or divide the numbers as if they were whole numbers. Finally put the decimal point into the answer so that the answer is close to your approximation.

$2.34 \times 2.6 \rightarrow$ approximation $2 \times 3 = 6$

```
    2 3 4
  ×   2 6
  1 4 0 4    (234 × 6)
  4 6 8 0    (234 × 20)
  6 0 8 4
```

→ so the answer must be **6.084**

$49.2 \div 4 \rightarrow$ approximation $48 \div 4 = 12$

```
  1 2 3
4)4 9 ¹2
```

→ so the answer must be **12.3**

1 Use a written method to answer these questions:

a) 35.4×2.8 ________ **b)** 2.6×36.7 ________ **c)** 2.85×7.4 ________

d) 9.37×5.9 ________ **e)** $85.6 \div 4$ ________ **f)** $109.6 \div 8$ ________

g) $239.22 \div 6$ ________ **h)** $2.94 \div 7$ ________

To check an answer to a calculation, work backwards from your answer using the inverse operation.

Here a division question is checked using multiplication:

49.2 $\div 4 \rightarrow$ approximation $48 \div 4 = 12$

```
  1 2 3
4)4 9 ¹2
```

→ so the answer must be **12.3**

CHECK

$12.3 \times 4 = (12 \times 4) + (0.3 \times 4)$

$= 48 + 1.2$

$= \mathbf{49.2}$

Check your answers to the calculations in question 1, using the inverse operation each time.

When solving a word problem, read it carefully and underline any key numbers. Decide what you will do. Make an approximation to get an idea of roughly what the answer might be. Then do the calculation. Remember to check your answer and see if it is sensible.

A school is arranging seats in rows in the hall. The hall is 10.48 metres wide. Corridors at least 1 m wide must be at both ends of a row and exactly in the middle of a row. Each chair is 55 cm wide. What is the maximum number of chairs that can fit in a row?

- Circle any key numbers.
- Decide what you will do →

subtract 3 metres for the row ends and the middle	10.48 m – 3 m
find the length of each half row	Ans ÷ 2
divide the answer by width of the chair (in metres)	Ans ÷ 0.55 m
round the answer down to the nearest whole chair and then multiply by 2	Ans × 2

- Make an approximation by rounding the numbers to get a rough idea. → about 14 chairs
- Now do the calculations.

10.48 – 3 = 7.48 m
7.48 ÷ 2 = 3.74
3.74 ÷ 0.55 m

6 . 8
55) **3 7 4 .**[44]**0**

6 chairs
6 × 2 = **12**

- Finally check that the answer is sensible. **12** chairs in a row

Practice

1 A table in a school canteen is 5.2 m long. Each chair in the canteen is 48 cm wide. How many chairs can fit along the length of both sides of this table?

____

2 A 10 m wide school staff room has a row of chairs that is 6 m long. Each chair in the row has a width of 75 cm. If the chairs are touching, how many chairs are in each row?

____

3 A school hall measures 11 m by 9 m. Chairs are arranged against the wall around all four sides of the hall, so that they touch each other. There are no seats at the very corners of the room and there is a 2 m gap for the door. Each chair has a length and width of 50 cm. How many chairs can fit around the hall?

____

4 In a school hall, chairs are arranged into 9 rows facing the front, with 14 chairs in each row. The seating area is 12 m from front to the back. Each chair is 45 cm from front to back.

a) How many people can be seated? __________

b) About how many centimetres of leg room will each row get, if the rows are evenly arranged?

____

How did I do?

	✔
I can add, subtract, multiply and divide on paper.	☐
I can solve word problems and check my answers.	☐

12: Simplifying expressions

In this unit you will revise:
- how to simplify or transform an expression by collecting like terms
- how to collect like terms including those in subtractions.

Start each revision session by trying to remember what you revised during your last one. If you have forgotten anything, go back and look at the topic again before starting a new topic.

What you should know

In Maths, letters are sometimes used to stand for numbers. It is quicker to write a letter, such as 'n', than to write out the words 'a number'. Here the letter 'n' stands for a number, the value of which is not yet known.

$n - 1$ is a short way of saying that 1 is subtracted from that number.

$n \times 9$ means the number is multiplied by 9.

n stands for a number. $2n$ means 2 lots of the number. $8n$ means 8 lots of the number.

Any letter of the alphabet can be used to stand for a number.

Get started

Simplifying means writing something more simply.

The **expression** $n + n + n$ can be written more simply as $3n$.

and $3n + n + 2n + 2n + n$ can be simplified as $9n$.

When an expression contains more than one letter you must find out how many of each letter there are. Don't mix the letters! Watch out also for whether to add or subtract:

$5a + 6b + 4b - 2a + a - b$ First count the 'a's $5a - 2a + a = 4a$

then count the 'b's $6b + 4b - b = 9b$

$5a + 6b + 4b - 2a + a - b = \mathbf{4a + 9b}$

This is called 'collecting like terms' which means grouping together things that are the same.

1 **Simplify** these expressions by collecting like terms (the first one has been done for you):

a) $g + 3g + 4h - h$ = **$4g + 3h$**

b) $5m - 2m + 2n - n + 3m$ = ________

c) $6x + 5y - 5x - 2y$ = ________

d) $9e + f + f - f - 4e$ = ________

e) $6c + 3d + c - 4c - d$ = ________

f) $7j + 3k - 2j + k - 2k$ = ________

g) $5p + 2q - q - 2p - 3p$ = ________

h) $7s + t + 2s - 5s - 2t$ = ________

i) $4a - 5a + b - 2b + 2a$ = ________

Some expressions use letters to stand for numbers but also include numbers called **constants**.

$2a + 7$ The 7 here is a constant because it is a known number and it doesn't change. This expression means 2 lots of an unknown number and then add 7.

$n + 3 + 2$ This means 3 and 2 are added to a number, and can be simplified as $n + 5$.

When simplifying expressions with letters and numbers, first count up how many of each letter there are and then add up the constants. Write them separately and remember to watch out for whether to add or subtract, like this:

$6a + 5b + 7 - 2a - 8b - 1$ Count the 'a's, then the 'b's and then add the constants.

$6a + 5b + 7 - 2a - 8b - 1 = \mathbf{4a - 3b + 6}$

Practice

1 **Simplify** these expressions by collecting like terms:

a) $a + 3a + b + c - 2b + 3c + a - 4a =$ ______________

b) $2p + 5q + q + r + 2r - p + p - 3q =$ ______________

c) $g + 3g + 3 + h + 4 - 2h - 2 =$ ______________

d) $m + 3 + 2m - 6 + 3n + n =$ ______________

e) $4 + 2c + 3d - c - 2 - 3d =$ ______________

f) $5s - 3t + 2 + 4t - 5 - 2s =$ ______________

g) $w + w - w + v - 2v + 7v + 2 + 6 - 5 =$ ______________

h) $2x - 5y + y + 7 + 3x + 5x + 2y - 4 + 1 =$ ______________

i) $2a + b + c + 3 + 2b - 3c - c + 4 + 6a - 5b + 2 - a + 2c =$ ______________

2 Add the expressions in two bricks next to each other (the first one has been done for you). Simplify your answer and write it in the brick above. Keep going until you have finished the pyramid.

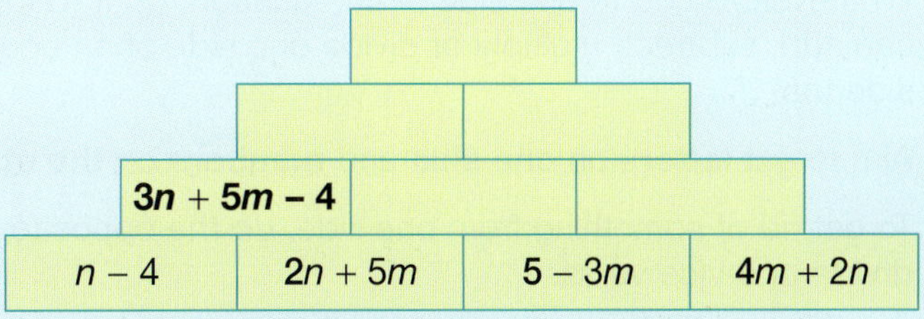

3 Find the perimeter of each shape and simplify the answer as much as possible.

a)

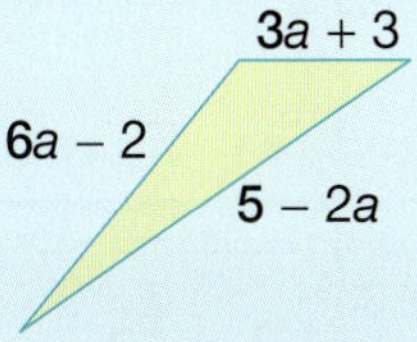

____

b)

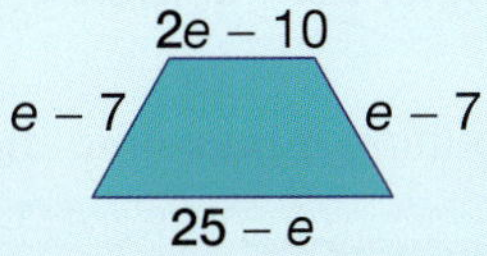

____

c)

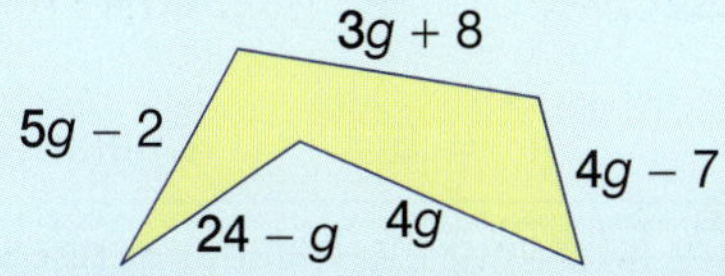

____

How did I do?

I know how to simplify or transform an expression by collecting like terms. ☐

I can collect like terms including those in subtractions. ☐

13: Equations

In this unit you will revise:
- solving equations with an unknown on either side
- solving equations with unknowns on both sides.

In an exam, look at the number of questions and keep an eye on how far through the exam you are. You will usually be told when you are half-way through so make sure that you are not working too slowly.

What you should know

Solving the equation means finding out what number a letter in an **equation** stands for. It is like cracking a code.

Look at each of these equations. Imagine a number is hidden underneath each letter. What number would this be to make each number sentence correct?

$a + 4 = 10$	$b - 2 = 7$	$5 \times c = 15$
a must be 6	***b*** must be 9	***c*** must be 3

An equation, such as **$8n + 4 = 44$**, can be solved to find the number, n.

There are two main ways that an equation can be solved, using ideas of **balancing** and using **inverses**. On this page the **balancing** method is used.

Get started

Both sides of an **equation** are worth the same – they **balance.**

$8n + 4 = 44$

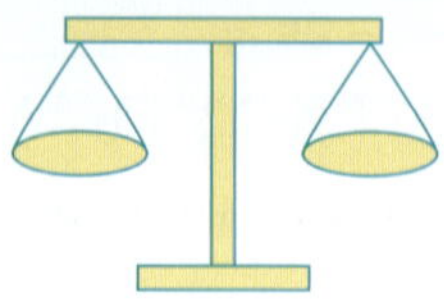

The balancing rules

1 Whatever you do to one side of an equation, do it to the other so that both sides still balance. So you can add, subtract, multiply or divide one side of an equation – but you must do the same to the other side too!

2 Aim to get **letters** on **one side** and **numbers** on **the other side**.

3 To get rid of something from one side, do the opposite. If it's an **add** then **subtract**, if it's a **times** then **divide** and vice versa.

$8n + 4 = 44$ (subtract 4 on both sides: -4, -4) (a) Get rid of the + 4 on the left. (Do the opposite – subtract 4 from both sides.)

$8n = 40$ (divide by 8 on both sides: $\div 8$, $\div 8$) (b) $8n$ means $n \times 8$. Get rid of the $\times 8$. (Do the opposite – divide by 8 on both sides.)

$n = 5$ Check your answer by putting it back into the equation.

1 Try following the balancing rules to solve these equations:

a) $2a + 3 = 19$ **b)** $3y + 15 = 24$ **c)** $7f - 12 = 16$ **d)** $4p + 2 = 14$

e) $35 = 3d + 5$ **f)** $28 = 4c - 4$ **g)** $35 = 5b - 5$ **h)** $32 = 6e + 8$

Sometimes an equation has letters on both sides of the equals sign, like this: $5y - 1 = 3y + 4$

To solve equations like these you need to follow the **balancing rules** to get the letters all on one side.

$5y - 1 = 3y + 4$ $-3y \quad\quad -3y$	(a) Get rid of the $3y$ on the right. (Do the opposite – subtract $3y$ from both sides.)
$2y - 1 = 4$ $+1 \quad\quad +1$	(b) Get rid of the -1 on the left. (Do the opposite – add 1 to both sides.)
$2y = 5$ $\div 2 \quad \div 2$	(c) $2n$ means $n \times 2$. Get rid of the x 2. (Do the opposite – divide by 2 on both sides.)
$y = 2.5$	Check your answer by putting it back into the equation.

2 Try following the balancing rules to solve these equations:

a) $6f - 13 = 3f - 4$ **b)** $5b - 4 = 3b + 6$ **c)** $6d - 3 = 2d + 7$

d) $6a - 2 = 4a + 8$ **e)** $10e - 6 = 4e + 9$ **f)** $9c - 4 = 8c + 1$

g) $4g + 1 = 3g + 8$ **h)** $5h - 5 = 3h + 2$ **i)** $7j - 1 = 4j + 8$

A common mistake that people make is to forget to write the letter after a subtraction.

This is **RIGHT**: $6a - 4a = 2a$. Think of it as **'6 lots of *a*'** subtract **'4 lots of *a*'** equals **'2 lots of *a*'**.

It is **WRONG** to write $6a - 4a = 2$.

Practice

1 Solve these equations:

a) $5r - 8 = 16 - r$ **b)** $4t + 2 = 2t + 6$ **c)** $8u - 6 = 6u - 2$

d) $9 - 3m = 2m + 4$ **e)** $10 + 2k = 7k - 5$ **f)** $20 - 2n = 3n - 10$

2 The lengths of these rectangles are shown as expressions. Write an equation for each rectangle and solve it. Use your answer to find the length of each rectangle.

a)

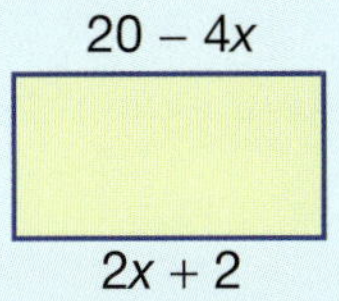

Length = ____________

b)

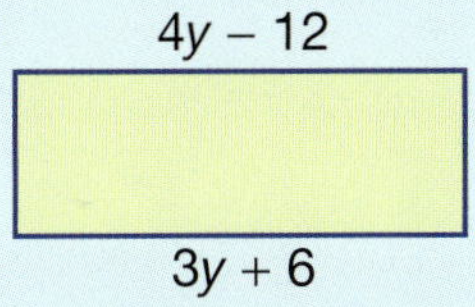

Length = ____________

c)

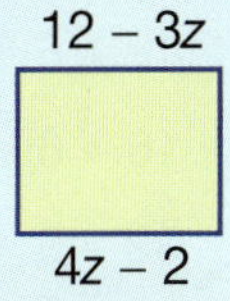

Length = ____________

How did I do?

	✔
I can solve an equation with an unknown on either side.	☐
I can solve an equation with unknowns on both sides.	☐

14: Formulae and substituting

In this unit you will revise:

- that algebraic operations follow the same order as arithmetic operations
- how to substitute integers into expressions involving small powers
- how to substitute integers into simple formulae and to find unknown values.

When using letters in Maths, be careful to write them clearly. It is easy to confuse the letter b with the number 6, z with 2 and s with 5 unless your handwriting is clear.

What you should know

To **substitute** means to exchange (or replace) one thing for another. In sport, players are substituted. In Maths, numbers are substituted for letters.

The expression $3y + 6$ means *'3 lots of a number and add 6'*. Remember that $3y$ means $3 \times y$.

You can substitute any number for the letter y: $3y + 6$

If **y is 5** then find *'3 lots of **5** and add 6'* $3 \times 5 + 6 = 15 + 6 = 21$

If **y is 8** then find *'3 lots of **8** and add 6'* $3 \times 8 + 6 = 24 + 6 = 30$

Get started

It is important to know that the order of doing calculations (**BODMAS** – see page 24) also applies to substitution. The **O** in **BODMAS** stands for **Other** operations such as using powers and roots. When an expression involves squares, cubes or roots, remember to work them out before division, multiplication, addition and subtraction.

If y is 5, then the value of $2y^2$ is found by first squaring 5 and then multiplying by 2, not the other way around.

$$2y^2 = 2 \times 25 = 50$$

The following expression has brackets, squaring, multiplication (by 2) and addition: $2(y - 1)^2 + 6$

If y is 5, then the value of the expression is found by working out the part in brackets first, then doing the squaring, then the multiplication and finally the addition.

$$y = 5 \qquad 2(y-1)^2 + 6 =$$
$$2(5-1)^2 + 6 =$$
$$2(4)^2 + 6 =$$
$$2 \times 16 + 6 =$$
$$32 + 6 = 38$$

1 Find the value of each expression, if $y = 2$.

a) $2(y + 3)^2 - 10$ ________ **b)** $10 - 2y^2$ ________ **c)** $(y - 1)^3$ ________

d) $(2y \times 2)^2 + 36$ ________ **e)** $4y^2 \times (6 - 2)$ ________ **f)** $5y^3 + 3 \times 2$ ________

g) $10 + 5y^2$ ________ **h)** $(3 + y^2) \times 2$ ________ **i)** $1 + \frac{y^2}{4}$ ________

Some expressions or formulae have more than one letter to substitute, like this: $2(1 + b^3) + 2a^2$

If $a = 3$ and $b = 2$ the value of the expression is:

$2(1 + 2^3) + 2 \times 3^2 =$

$2(1 + 8) + 2 \times 9 =$

$2 \times 9 + 2 \times 9 = 18 + 18 =$ **36**

The following formula shows a relationship between the number of faces, F, edges, E, and vertices, V, of polyhedrons (3-D shapes with straight sides):

$E = F + V - 2$

By substituting the number of faces and vertices, the number of edges can be found.

2 Use the formula $E = F + V - 2$ to find the number of edges of each shape.

a) Cuboid: $F = 6$ and $V = 8$,
$E =$ __________

b) Triangular prism: $F = 5$ and $V = 6$,
$E =$ __________

c) Square pyramid: $F = 5$ and $V = 5$,
$E =$ __________

d) Hexagonal prism: $F = 8$ and $V = 12$,
$E =$ __________

e) Tetrahedron: $F = 4$ and $V = 4$,
$E =$ __________

f) Pentagonal pyramid: $F = 6$ and $V = 6$,
$E =$ __________

Practice

1 This grid shows different expressions which use the letters a and b. Substitute the following values of a and b into each expression.

Write the value of each expression in the corresponding sections of the grids below.

$2b^3 + 3$	$3(a^2 + b^3)$	$1 - a^2$
$a^2 + 3b^3 + 5$	$2(1 - b^3 - a^2)$	$3a^2 - 3$
$a^2 - 4$	$a^2 + 2$	$b^3 + 6$

a) Let $a = 3$ and $b = 2$

19		

b) Let $a = 4$ and $b = 1$

c) Let $a = 5$ and $b = 3$

2 The formula for the **surface area**, S, of a cuboid with length, l, breadth, b, and height, h, is:

$\mathbf{S = 2bl + 2lh + 2hb}$

Find the surface area for a cuboid with these dimensions:

a) $l = 6$ cm, $b = 5$ cm, $h = 10$ cm __________

b) $l = 7$ cm, $b = 2$ cm, $h = 5$ cm __________

c) $l = 5$ cm, $b = 3$ cm, $h = 7$ cm __________

d) $l = 9$ cm, $b = 6$ cm, $h = 14$ cm __________

How did I do?

	✔
I know that algebraic operations follow the same order as arithmetic operations.	☐
I can substitute integers into expressions involving small powers.	☐
I can substitute integers into simple formulae and find unknown values.	☐

15: Sequences

In this unit you will revise:

- how to describe sequences using term-to-term and position-to-term rules
- how to generate sequences using position-to-term rules
- describing the *n*th term of a sequence.

Don't leave revision to just before a test or exam. Students who do well usually have worked hard throughout the year.

What you should know

Each number in a **sequence** is called a **term.** It is important to be able to say which term in a sequence you are talking about.

1, 4, 9, 16, 25, 36, ... The **third term** in this sequence is **9**.

The **fifth term** in this sequence is **25**.

Sequences can be ascending or descending. **Ascending** sequences are those where the terms in the sequence get larger. **Descending** sequences are those where the terms in the sequence get smaller. Sequences can increase (go up) or decrease (go down) by the same-sized steps, like these:

1, 3, 5, 7, 9, 11, ... **8, 6, 4, 2, 0, −2, −4, ...**

Or they can increase or decrease by different-sized steps, like these:

1, 4, 9, 16, 25, 36, ... **32, 16, 8, 4, 2, 1, ...**

There are two ways of describing sequences: using the **term-to-term** rule or the **position-to-term** rule. The **term-to-term** rule describes the first term and explains how each term is different from the previous term.

3, 7, 11, 15, 19, 23, ... The first term is 3. Each term increases by 4.

Get started

The **position-to-term** rule explains how you can work out each term from where it is in the sequence, its position. Write position numbers, starting at 1, above the sequence.

position number:	1	2	3	4	5	6	
terms of sequence:	3,	7,	11,	15,	19,	23,	...

The **position-to-term** rule can be described in words:

Multiply the position number by 4 and subtract 1.

It can also be written in symbols:

nth term = $4n - 1$

Each term can be generated by following the rule:

1st term	2nd term	3rd term	4th term	5th term	
$1 \times 4 - 1 = 3$	$2 \times 4 - 1 = 7$	$3 \times 4 - 1 = 11$	$4 \times 4 - 1 = 15$	$5 \times 4 - 1 = 19$	...

We can use the **position-to-term** rule to predict other numbers in the sequence, such as the 10th term. Follow the rule for the position number 10.

10th term

$10 \times 4 - 1 = 39$ → The 10th number in the sequence will be 39.

1 Write the first **five** terms of these sequences:

a) Multiply the position number by 4 and add 3 — nth term $= 4n + 3$

position number (n):	1	2	3	4	5	
terms of sequence:	____	____	____	____	____	...

b) Multiply the position number by 3 and subtract 5 — nth term $= 3n - 5$

position number (n):	1	2	3	4	5	
terms of sequence:	____	____	____	____	____	...

c) Multiply the position number by 5 and subtract the answer from 20 — nth term $= 20 - 5n$

position number (n):	1	2	3	4	5	
terms of sequence:	____	____	____	____	____	...

To find the **position-to-term** rule, or the rule for the nth term as it is sometimes called, look for a pattern between each position number and its related term.

position number (n):	1	2	3	4	5	6	
terms of sequence:	3,	6,	9,	12,	15,	18,	...

Here you can see that you multiply the position number by 3.

So the rule in symbols is nth term $= 3n$

2 Write the rule for the nth term for each sequence and state the 10th term of the sequence:

a)

position number (n):	1	2	3	4	5	6	
terms of sequence:	5,	10,	15,	20,	25,	30,	...

nth term = ____ 10th term = ____

b)

position number (n):	1	2	3	4	5	6	
terms of sequence:	4,	8,	12,	16,	20,	24,	...

nth term = ____ 10th term = ____

Practice

1 Count how many squares each shape is made from to create a sequence.

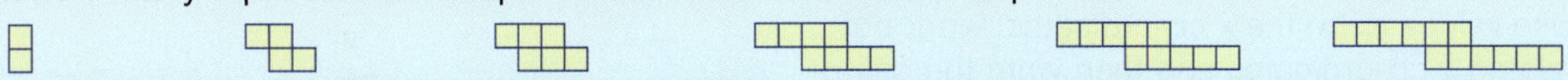

a) ____ ____ ____ ____ ____ ____

b) Write the rule for the nth term in symbols nth term = ____

c) Write the number of squares used to make the 10th shape in the sequence 10th term = ____

2 Generate the first five terms of each of these sequences:

a) nth term $= 5n + 1$ ____ ____ ____ ____ ____

b) nth term $= 2n + 2$ ____ ____ ____ ____ ____

c) nth term $= 10 - n$ ____ ____ ____ ____ ____

How did I do?

	✔
I know how to describe sequences using term-to-term and position-to-term rules.	☐
I can generate sequences using position-to-term rules.	☐
I can describe the nth term of a sequence.	☐

16: Straight line graphs

In this unit you will revise:

- how to plot straight line graphs, where y is given explicitly in terms of x
- how functions of the form $y = mx + c$ correspond to straight line graphs.

When making your own revision notes, use different colours to show different things. Write some note about straight line graphs. You could use one colour each time you write an x co-ordinate and a different colour for the y co-ordinate.

What you should know

Co-ordinates are written as pairs of numbers inside brackets, like (**3**, **2**). The first number tells you how many across from zero to move and the second number tells you how many up or down to move.

The first number is called the ***x* co-ordinate** and the second number is called the ***y* co-ordinate**, (***x***, ***y***).

Functions can be drawn as lines on a co-ordinate grid. Linear functions are those that produce straight lines. All **horizontal** lines on a grid are called **'*y* = a number'**. To find what the number is, see where the line crosses the ***y* axis**.

All **vertical** lines on a grid are called **'*x* = a number'**. To find what the number is, see where the line crosses the ***x* axis**.

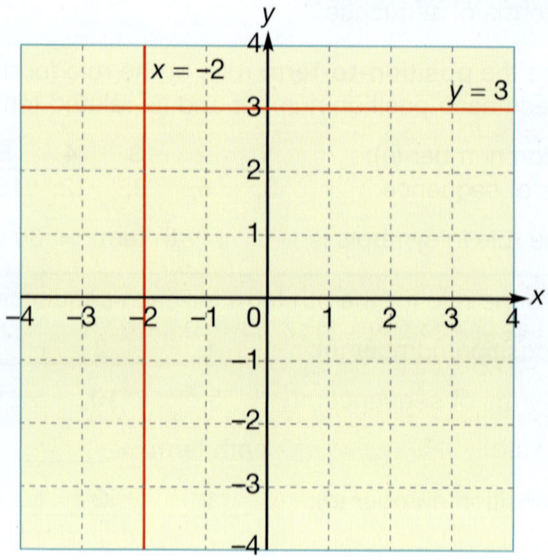

Get started

Sets of co-ordinates can be generated by following a rule, written in words or using letters:

Rule in words: *'Multiply the x co-ordinate by 2 and add 1 to make the y co-ordinate'*
Rule using letters: $y = 2x + 1$

Choose values to be the x co-ordinates, work out the related y co-ordinates and then write the pair of co-ordinates in brackets.

The co-ordinates can be written into a table like this:

$y = 2x + 1$					
x	–2	–1	0	1	2
y	–3	–1	1	3	5

These are the pairs of co-ordinates:

(–2, –3), (–1, –1), (0, 1), (1, 3) and (2, 5)

The pairs of co-ordinates form a straight line on the grid.

The pairs of co-ordinates of *every* point that lies on this straight line can be generated using the same rule, $y = 2x + 1$. The rule is called the equation or function of the straight line or its **linear function**.

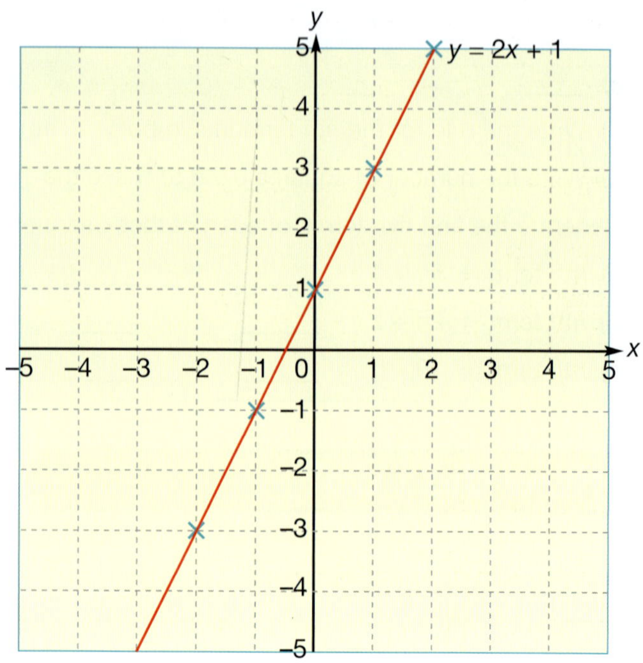

1 **a)** Fill in the missing y co-ordinates in the table for the rule $1 - 2x = y$ and write the pairs of co-ordinates produced.

$1 - 2x = y$					
x	−2	−1	0	1	2
y	5				

(______) (______) (______) (______) (______)

b) Plot the pairs of co-ordinates on the previous graph and label the line correctly.

All lines on a grid are vertical, horizontal or diagonal. The diagonal lines have functions in the form

$\boldsymbol{y} = m\boldsymbol{x} + c$ where m and c are numbers.

$y = 3x + 4$ → m is 3 and c is 4

$y = -2x - 3$ → m is −2 and c is −3

$y = x - 2$ → m is 1 and c is −2

$y = 4x$ → m is 4 and c is 0

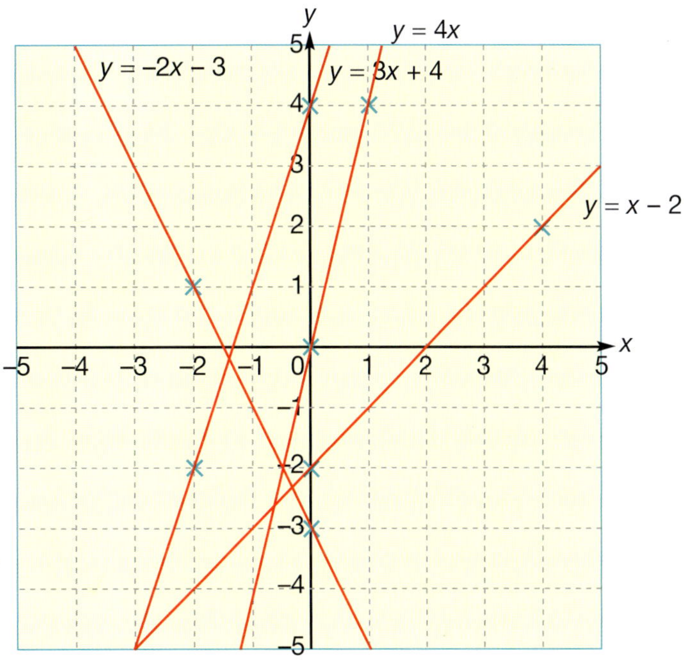

The gradient of a straight line on the graph (how steep it is) is the value of m.

The point where the line crosses the y axis (the intercept) is the value of c.

The line $y = 3x + 4$ has a gradient of 3 and its intercept with the y axis is at the y co-ordinate 4.

A positive gradient means that the line slopes up to the right. A negative gradient means that it slopes up to the left. When two lines have the same gradient they are **parallel** to each other.

Practice

1 State the gradient and the y co-ordinate of the intercept of the line for each of these functions:

a) $y = 3x - 1$

Gradient = ________ Intercept = ________

b) $y = -2x + 4$

Gradient = ________ Intercept = ________

c) $y = 8x$

Gradient = ________ Intercept = ________

d) $y = x - 2$

Gradient = ________ Intercept = ________

How did I do?

	✔
I can plot straight line graphs.	☐
I can find the gradient of a line when given a function in the form $y = mx + c$.	☐
I can find the intercept of a line when given a function in the form $y = mx + c$.	☐

17: Test 2

1 If $b = 4$ find the values of:

a) $5b^2$ ________ **b)** $4b^2$ ________ **c)** $2b^2 - 2$ ________

d) $\frac{\sqrt{b}}{2}$ ________ **e)** $\frac{4 \times \sqrt{b}}{8}$ ________ **f)** $\frac{2b^2}{\sqrt{b}}$ ________

g) $19 + b^2$ ________ **h)** $b + b^2 + \sqrt{b} \times 5$ ________ **i)** $1 + \frac{b^2}{8}$ ________

2 Work out the correct answers for these questions. Remember to use the order of **BODMAS**.

a) $\frac{44 - 12}{52 + 12}$ ________ **b)** $\frac{\sqrt{36} + 94}{5 \times 5}$ ________

c) $\frac{(1 + 7)^2}{(13 - 9)^2}$ ________ **d)** $\frac{\sqrt{49} \times 2^3}{4 \times \sqrt{4}}$ ________

3 Use a written method to answer these questions:

a) 13.6×4.8 ________ **b)** 3.6×44.4 ________ **c)** 2.52×7.8 ________

d) 9.63×2.9 ________ **e)** $64.2 \div 3$ ________ **f)** $123.3 \div 9$ ________

g) $199.35 \div 5$ ________ **h)** $2.52 \div 6$ ________

4 A table in a school canteen is 5.05 m long. Each chair in the canteen is 45 cm wide. How many chairs can fit along the length of both sides of this table?

____

5 Add the expressions in two bricks next to each other (the first one has been done for you). Simplify your answer and write it in the brick above. Keep going until you have finished the pyramid.

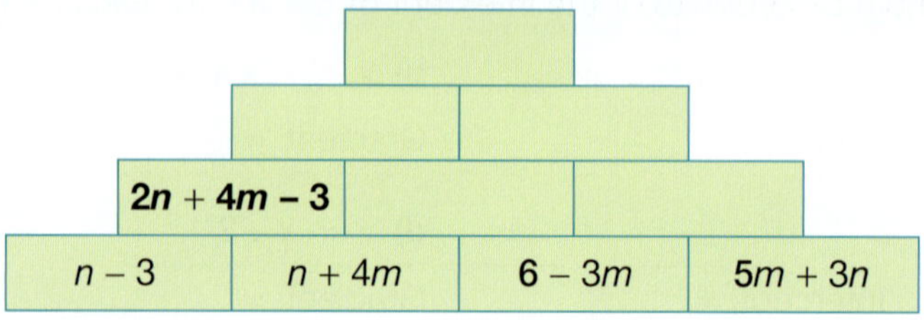

6 Find the perimeter of each shape and simplify the answer as much as possible.

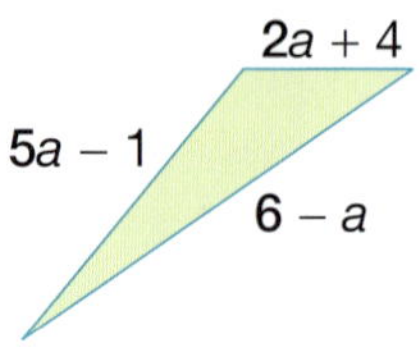

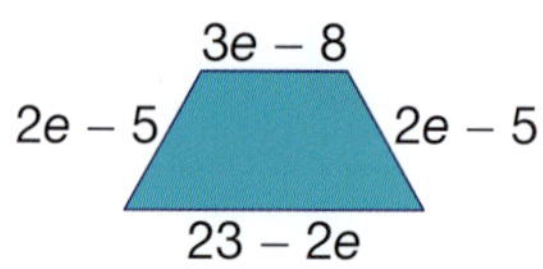

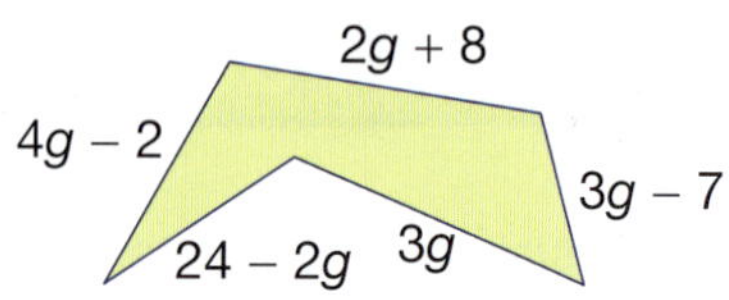

________ ________ ________

7 Try following the balancing rules to solve these equations:

a) $6a + 4 = 76$ b) $3y + 2 = 32$ c) $4f - 4 = 0$ d) $5p + 7 = 32$

e) $32 = 4d + 4$ f) $5 = 2c - 3$ g) $25 = 3b - 5$ h) $31 = 6e + 7$

8 Solve these equations:

a) $3r + 4 = 4r + 4$ b) $t + 7 = 6t + 17$ c) $7u - 3 = 5u - 33$

d) $8 - 6m = 3 - 7m$ e) $1 + 5k = k + 17$ f) $1 - 2n = 5n - 6$

9 This grid shows different expressions which use the letters *a* and *b*.

Substitute the following values of *a* and *b* into each expression. Write the value of each expression in the corresponding sections of the grid below.

Let $a = 6$ and $b = 4$

$2b^3 + 3$	$3(a^2 + b^3)$	$1 - a^2$
$a^2 + 3b^3 + 5$	$2(1 - b^3 - a^2)$	$3a^2 - 3$
$a^2 - 4$	$a^2 + 2$	$b^3 + 6$

10 Generate the first five terms of each of these sequences:

a) *n*th term $= 6n + 1$ _______ _______ _______ _______ _______

b) *n*th term $= 4n - 2$ _______ _______ _______ _______ _______

c) *n*th term $= 8 - n$ _______ _______ _______ _______ _______

11 State the gradient and the *y* co-ordinate of the intercept of the line for each of these equations:

a) $y = 2x - 1$

Gradient = _______ Intercept = _______

b) $y = -3x + 5$

Gradient = _______ Intercept = _______

c) $y = 5x$

Gradient = _______ Intercept = _______

d) $y = x - 4$

Gradient = _______ Intercept = _______

18: Area

In this unit you will revise:
- the formulae for the area of a triangle, parallelogram and trapezium
- how to calculate areas of compound shapes.

What you should know

Area is the amount of surface that a shape covers. In a 2-D shape (flat shape) it is the space inside the lines or within a boundary. In a 3-D shape (solid shape) it is the total amount of surface of all the faces. Area is measured in square units like square centimetres (cm^2) or square metres (m^2).

For 3-D shapes this is often called **surface area**.

Here is the formula for the area, A, of a rectangle with length (l) and width (w): $\boldsymbol{A = l \times w}$

Get started

The diagrams below show that the area of a triangle is half the area of a rectangle.

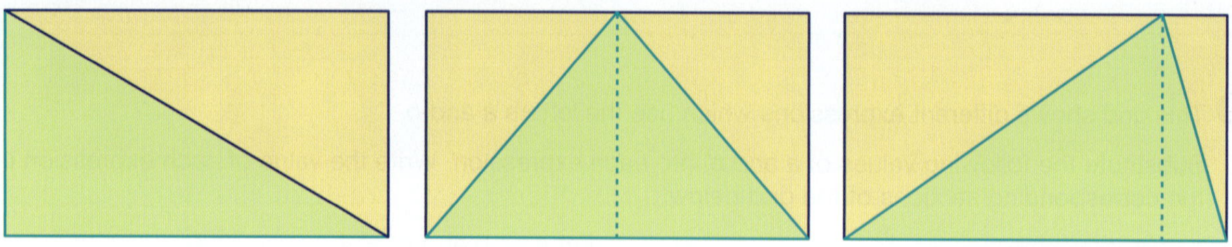

This can be written as a formula for the area, A, of a triangle with base (b) and height (h):

$\boldsymbol{A = \frac{1}{2}b \times h}$ or $\boldsymbol{A = (b \times h) \div 2}$

Note that the height is the **perpendicular** height, not the length of a sloping side of the triangle.

1 Find the area of each triangle. Be careful as some measurements have been given that you will not need to use.

a)

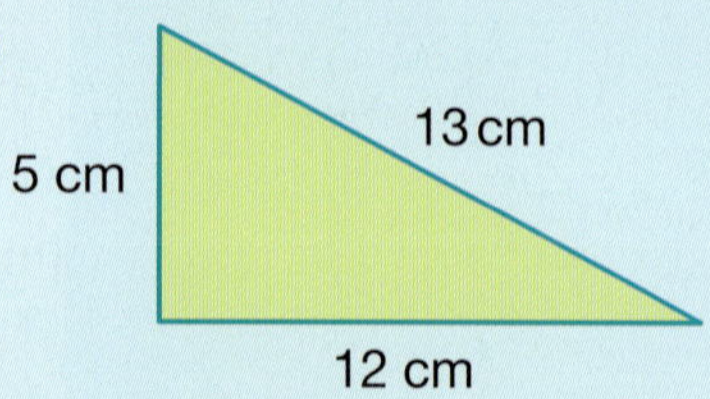

Area = __________ cm^2

b)

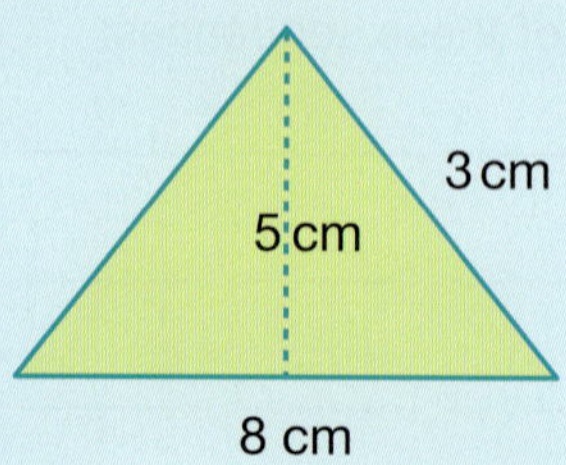

Area = __________ cm^2

c)

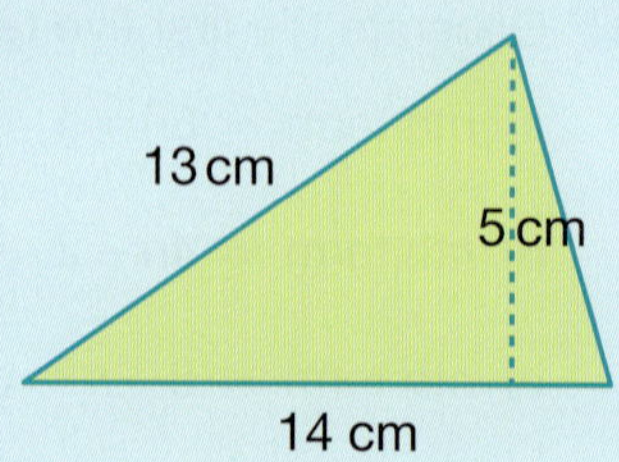

Area = __________ cm^2

d)

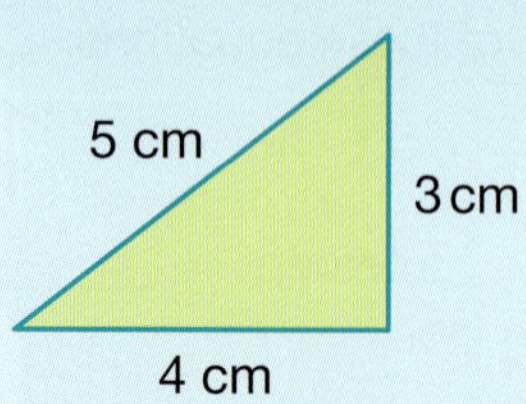

Area = __________ cm^2

e)

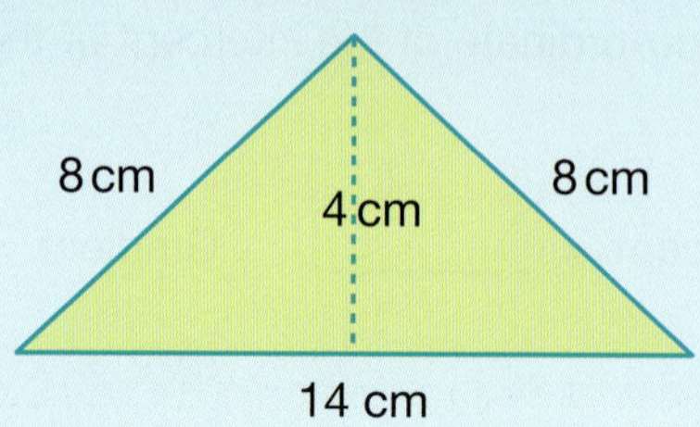

Area = __________ cm^2

f)

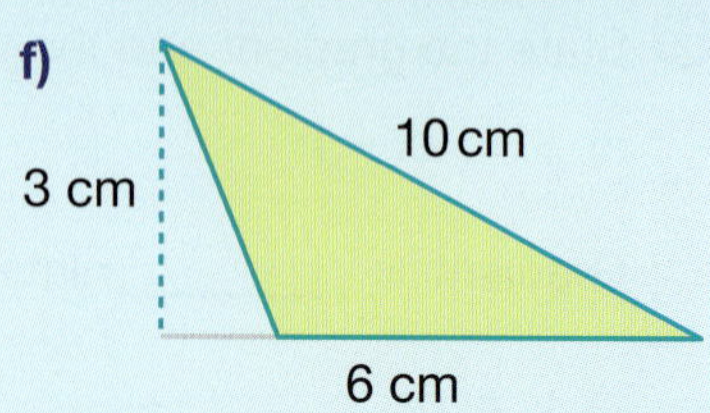

Area = __________ cm^2

These are the formulae for the area of a parallelogram and a trapezium:

Parallelogram

Area = base × perpendicular height

$\boldsymbol{A = b \times h}$

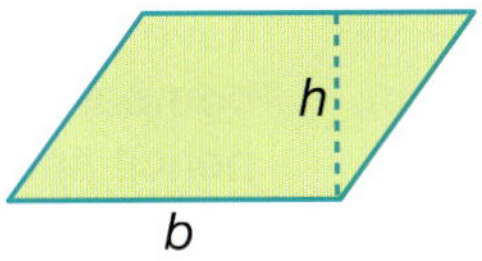

Trapezium

Area = $\frac{1}{2}$(sum of parallel sides) × perpendicular height

$\boldsymbol{A = \frac{1}{2}(a + b) \times h}$

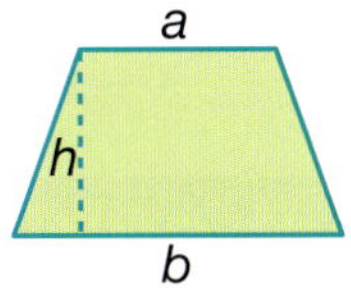

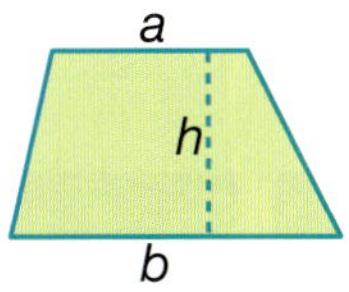

2 Find the area of each shape. Be careful as some shapes have been rotated.

a)

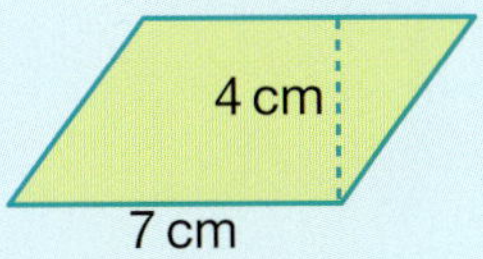

Area = ________ cm^2

b)

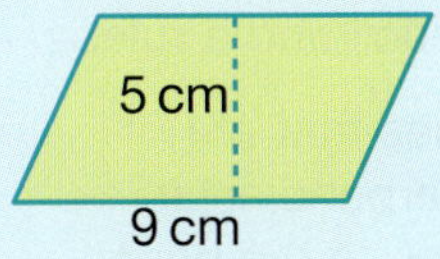

Area = ________ cm^2

c)

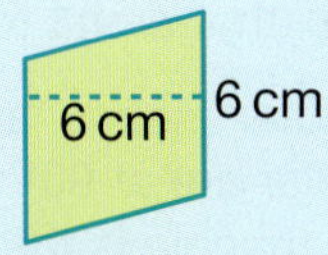

Area = ________ cm^2

d)

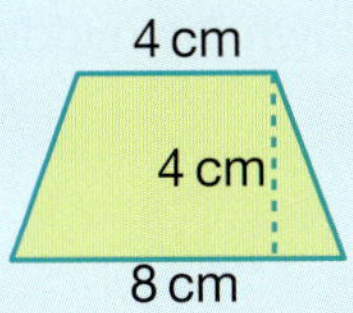

Area = ________ cm^2

e)

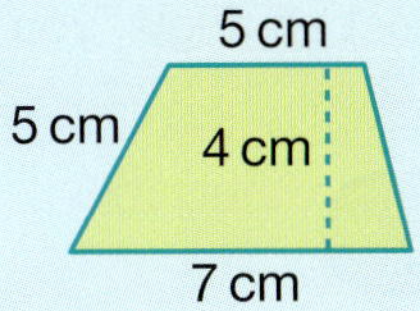

Area = ________ cm^2

f)

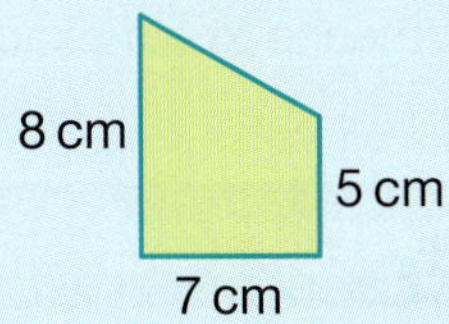

Area = ________ cm^2

When finding the area of something made from more than one shape, split it into parts and find the area of each part first before adding them all together to find the total area. You may also need to work out the lengths of unmarked sides.

Practice

1 Find the area of each shape by splitting it into parts.

a)

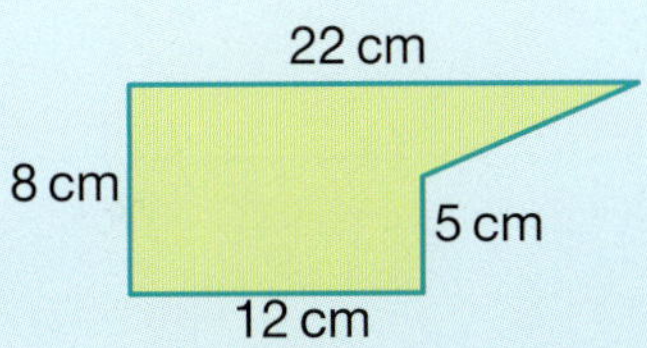

Area = ________ cm^2

b)

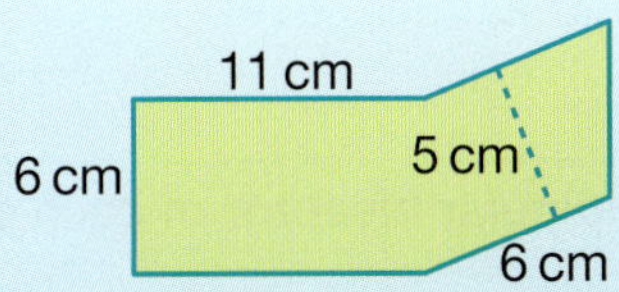

Area = ________ cm^2

c)

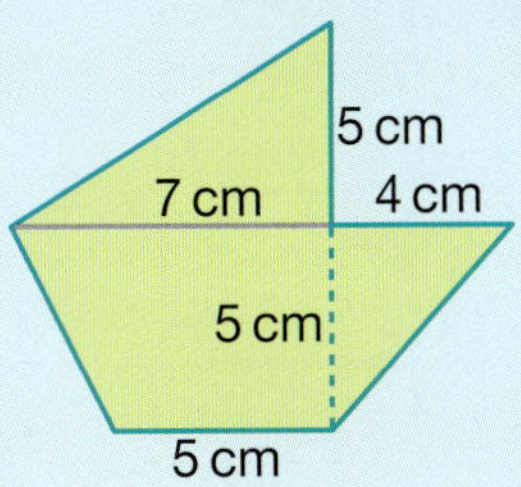

Area = ________ cm^2

d)

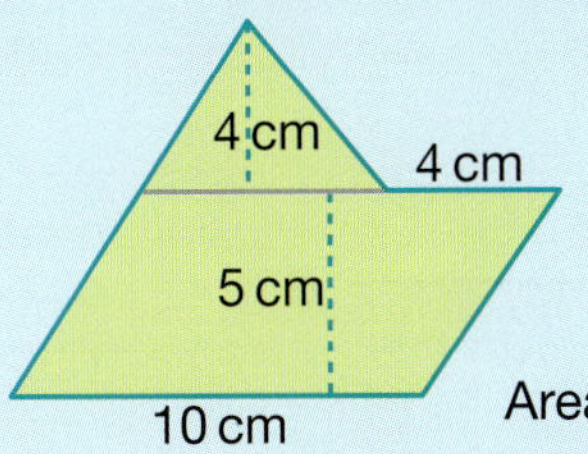

Area = ________ cm^2

How did I do?

	✔
I know the formulae for the area of a triangle, parallelogram and trapezium.	☐
I can calculate the areas of triangles, parallelograms and trapeziums.	☐
I can calculate the area of compound shapes.	☐

19: Construction

In this unit you will revise:
- how to construct the perpendicular bisector of a line
- how to construct a bisector of an angle.

Make sure your pencil case has all the right equipment. Make sure that you have a good pair of compasses, a sharp pencil and a ruler.

What you should know

These pages are about construction: drawing shapes and lines accurately. You will need a pair of compasses (that aren't too loose), a sharp pencil and a ruler.

Perpendicular means 'at right angles to'. Lines that are perpendicular are at 90° to each other. The perpendicular height of a triangle is the height, at right angles to the base, shown here as a dotted line:

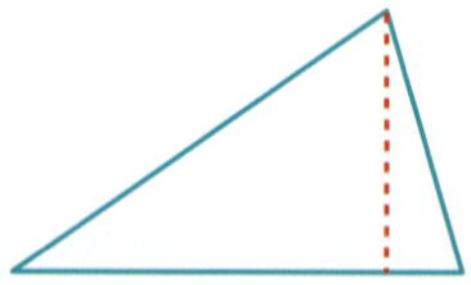

To **bisect** means to cut exactly in half. If you bisect an angle, you split it exactly in half down the middle.

Get started

To 'construct the perpendicular bisector of a line' means to draw another line at right angles to it exactly in the middle. To do this, follow these instructions:

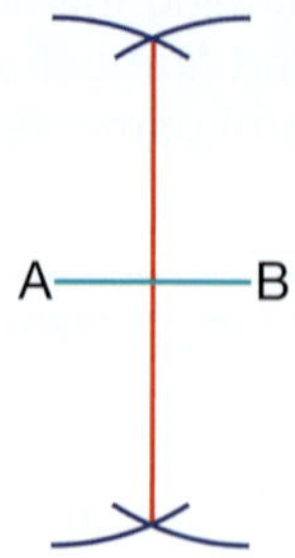

- **Start with the line AB**.
- Make sure the compasses are wider than half the length of the line. Put the point on A and draw two arc lines, one above and one below the line AB.
- Keeping the compasses set at the same width, lift the point and place it on B. Draw two arc lines that cross the previous ones.
- Finally use the ruler to draw a straight line exactly through the points where the arc lines cross.

1 Construct the **perpendicular bisector** of each of these lines:

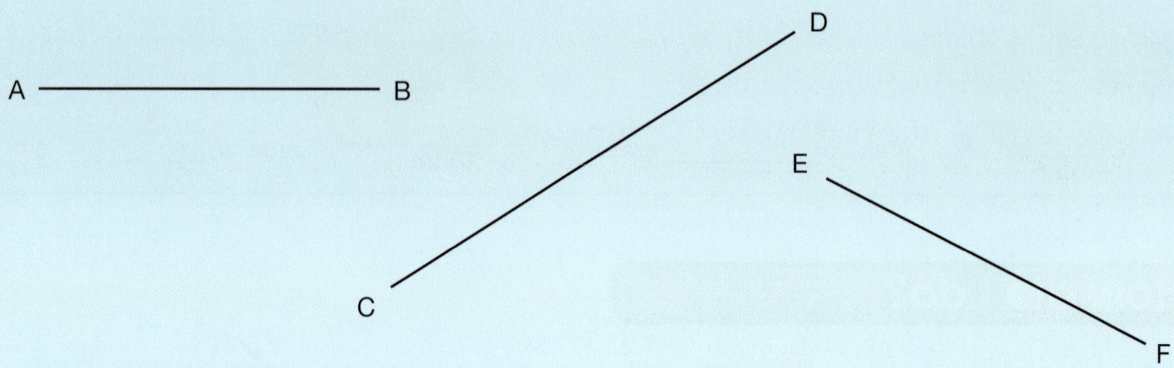

To construct the bisector of an angle means to split the angle exactly in half. To do this, follow these instructions:

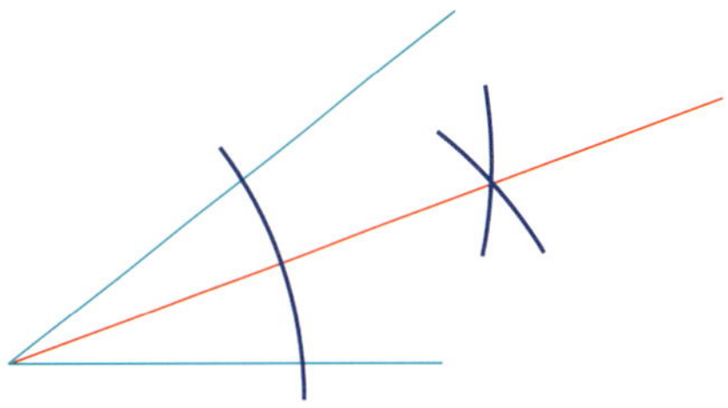

- **Start with the angle**.
- Put the point of the compasses on the corner of the angle and draw a large arc that crosses both lines of the angle.
- Lift the point and place it on the point where the large arc crosses one of the lines. Draw a small arc line.
- Keeping the compasses set at the same width, lift the point and place it where the arc crosses the other line. Draw a small arc line to cross the other one.
- Finally use the ruler to draw a straight line from the corner of the angle to where the arc lines cross.

2 Construct the **bisector** of each of these angles.

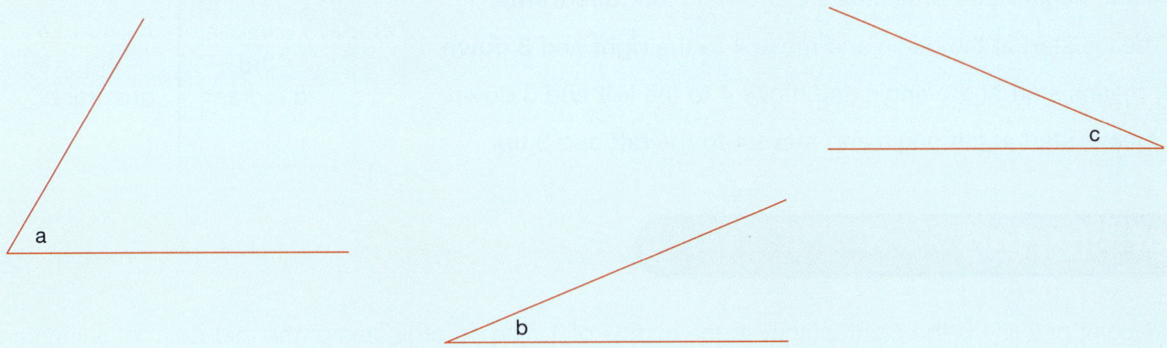

Practice

1 On paper, draw four lines at different orientations on the page.

a) On each, draw the perpendicular bisector.

b) Then join the ends of the original line to the places where the arcs cross to make a **rhombus**, like this:

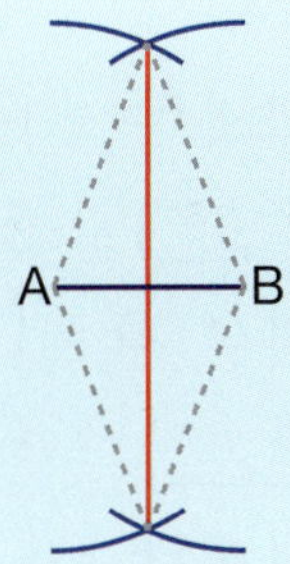

2 On paper, draw angles in different orientations on the page.

a) On each, draw the bisector of the angle.

b) Then join the points where the large arc crosses the lines of the angle to the places where the small arcs cross to make a **rhombus**, like this:

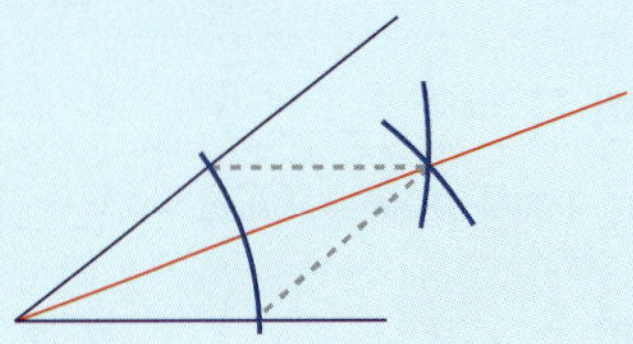

How did I do?

	✔
I can construct the perpendicular bisector of a line.	☐
I can construct a bisector of an angle.	☐

20: Co-ordinates

In this unit you will revise:
- plotting co-ordinates in all four quadrants
- how to find the co-ordinates of a mid-point along a line.

What you should know

The **origin** is the point (0, 0) on a co-ordinate grid.

Co-ordinates are written as pairs of numbers inside brackets, like (**3**, **2**). The first number, the ***x* co-ordinate,** tells you how many across from the origin to move and the second number, the ***y* co-ordinate**, tells you how many up or down to move.

Positive and negative co-ordinates are shown in four **quadrants.**

(4, –3) means start at the origin and move **4** to the **right** and **3 down**.

(–4, –3) means start at the origin and move **4** to the **left** and **3 down**.

(–4, 3) means start at the origin and move **4** to the **left** and **3 up**.

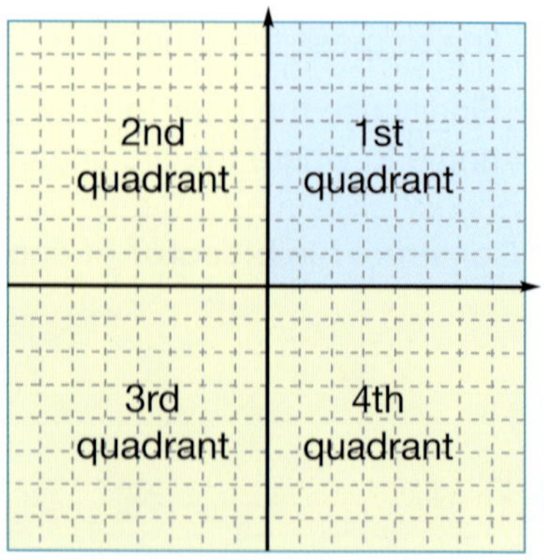

Get started

The mid-point of a line is the point exactly in the middle of it. The co-ordinates of the mid-point of a line can be found. On the grid below is the line AB. The mid-point is the point exactly half-way between A and B.

1 Write the co-ordinates of the letters in each pair. Join the two points on the grid with a line. Mark the mid-point of the line and give its co-ordinates. One has been done for you.

a) A = **(–1, 4)** B = **(5, 4)**
mid-point of AB = **(2, 4)**

b) C = (__, __) D = (__, __)
mid-point of CD = (__, __)

c) E = (__, __) F = (__, __)
mid-point of EF = (__, __)

d) C = (__, __) E = (__, __)
mid-point of CE = (__, __)

e) B = (__, __) H = (__, __)
mid-point of BH = (__, __)

f) F = (__, __) G = (__, __)
mid-point of FG = (__, __)

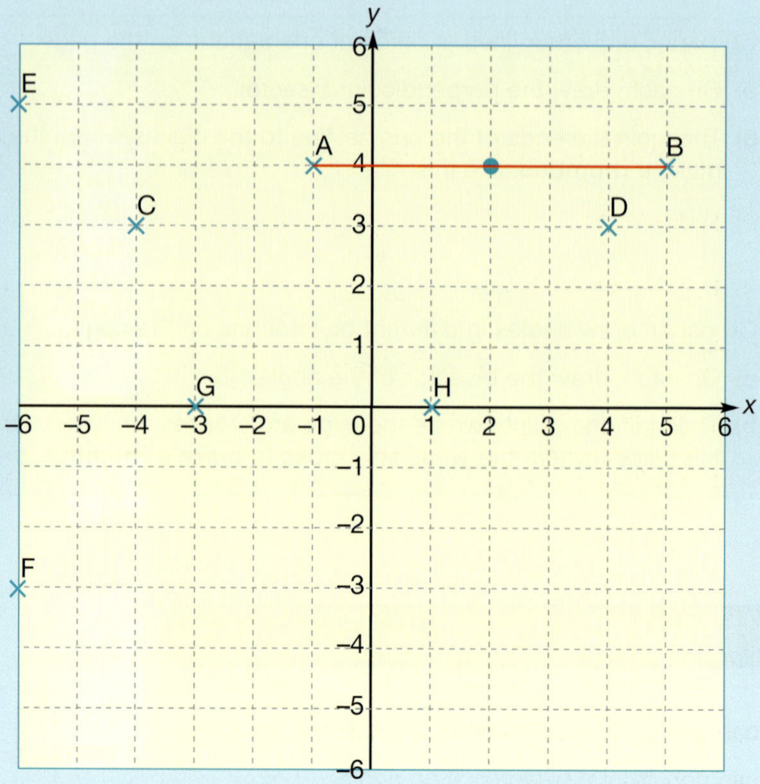

There is a formula for finding the co-ordinates of the mid-point of a line. If the end-points of the line have the co-ordinates (x_1, y_1) and (x_2, y_2) then:

- the x co-ordinate of the mid-point is $\frac{1}{2}(x_1 + x_2)$
- the y co-ordinate of the mid-point is $\frac{1}{2}(y_1 + y_2)$.

Or put in another way:

- To find the x co-ordinate of the mid-point: add the x co-ordinates and halve the answer.
- To find the y co-ordinate of the mid-point: add the y co-ordinates and halve the answer.

So for a line with the end-points (2, 3) and (–4, –3)

The x co-ordinate of the mid-point is:

$\frac{1}{2}(2 + -4) = \frac{1}{2}(-2) = -1$

The y co-ordinate of the mid-point is:

$\frac{1}{2}(3 + -3) = \frac{1}{2}(0) = 0$

So the mid-point has co-ordinates (–1, 0).

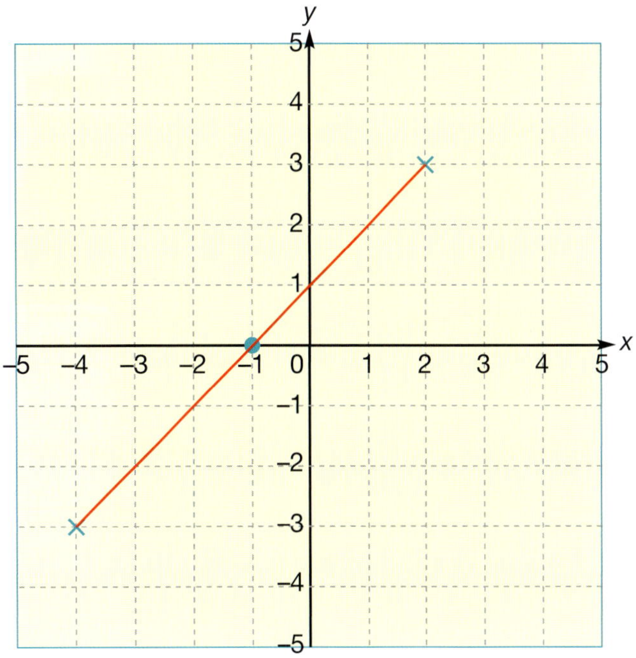

2 Find the co-ordinates of the mid-point (M) of the line PQ if the co-ordinates of P and Q are as follows:

a) P (–2, 3) Q (4, –1) M = (__,__)
b) P (–3, –2) Q (1, –4) M = (__,__)
c) P (–3, 0) Q (3, –4) M = (__,__)
d) P (–1, –3) Q (–5, 5) M = (__,__)

3 Check your answers by plotting each of the pairs of points P and Q and finding their mid-point on the grid above.

Practice

1 Find the co-ordinates of the mid-point (M) of the line PQ if the co-ordinates of P and Q are as follows:

a) P (5, –9) Q (–3, 5) M = (__,__)
b) P (–3, –7) Q (5, 7) M = (__,__)
c) P (–6, 4) Q (8, –8) M = (__,__)
d) P (–8, –3) Q (0, 5) M = (__,__)
e) P (–8, –6) Q (4, 4) M = (__,__)
f) P (–2, 7) Q (8, –3) M = (__,__)
g) P (–1, –4) Q (9, –6) M = (__,__)
h) P (–5, –2) Q (7, –8) M = (__,__)
i) P (–6, 2) Q (5, –4) M = (__,__)
j) P (–5, 0) Q (4, –6) M = (__,__)

How did I do?

	✔
I can plot and read co-ordinates in all four quadrants.	☐
I can find the co-ordinates of a mid-point along a line.	☐

21: 2-D shape

In this unit you will revise:
- what congruent means
- how to recognise congruent shapes
- the names and properties of 2-D shapes.

What you should know

Here are some 2-D shapes (polygons) you should know:

Triangle: 3 straight sides	**Quadrilateral**: 4 straight sides	**Pentagon**: 5 straight sides
Hexagon: 6 straight sides	**Heptagon**: 7 straight sides	**Octagon**: 8 straight sides
Nonagon: 9 straight sides	**Decagon**: 10 straight sides	**Dodecagon**: 12 straight sides

A shape is said to be **regular** when all its sides are the same length and all its angles are the same size.

To **bisect** means to split something exactly in half. When diagonals of a shape bisect each other they cross at their mid-points, like this:

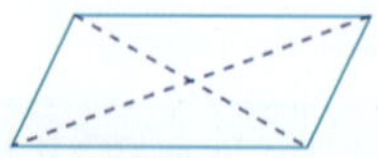

Get started

Two shapes are said to be **congruent** when they are identical in **size and shape**. They do not, however, need to be in the same orientation, they can be rotated, translated or reflected. These two shapes are congruent. The corresponding angles and sides are the same.

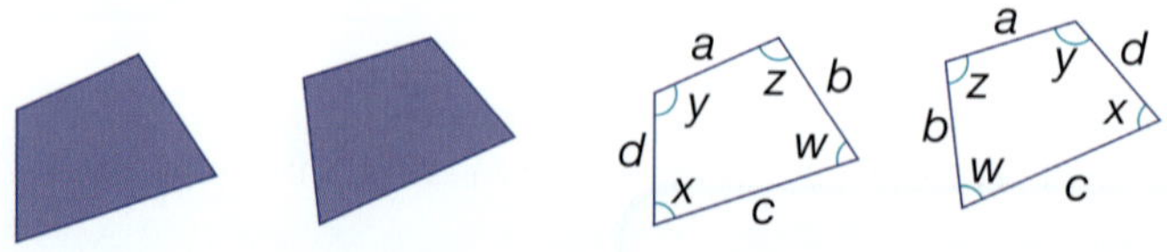

1 Tick the shapes in each row that are congruent to the blue shape:

a)

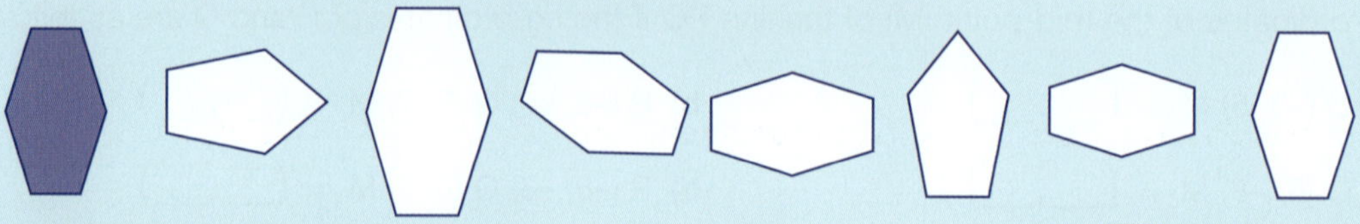

b)

c)

d)

A **parallelogram** is a type of **quadrilateral**.
Its opposite sides are equal and parallel.
Its diagonals **bisect** each other.

A **rhombus** is a parallelogram with four equal sides.
Its diagonals **bisect** at right angles.
Both diagonals are lines of symmetry.
It has a rotational symmetry of order 2.

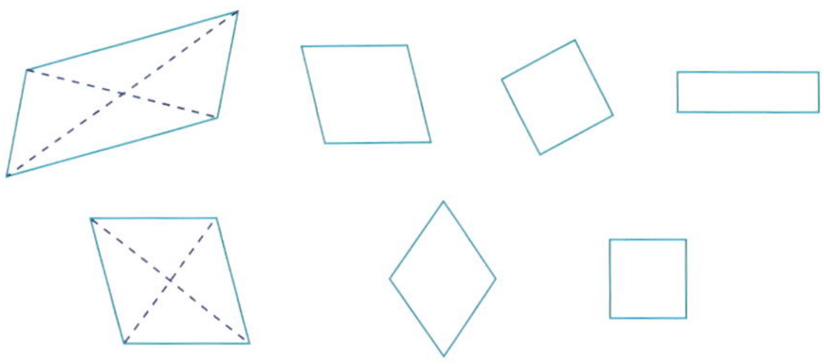

2 Tick whether each sentence is true or false when describing the properties of a kite.

A **kite** is a quadrilateral that has two pairs of adjacent sides that are equal	True ☐	False ☐
Its diagonals **bisect** each other.	True ☐	False ☐
Its diagonals cross at right angles.	True ☐	False ☐
Its diagonals are the same length.	True ☐	False ☐
One diagonal is a line of symmetry.	True ☐	False ☐
It has two lines of symmetry.	True ☐	False ☐
It has a rotational symmetry of order 2.	True ☐	False ☐

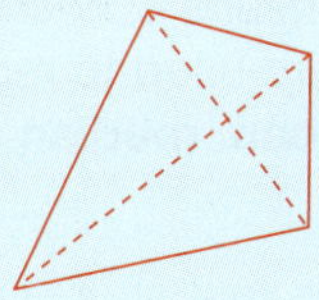

3 Tick whether each sentence is true or false when describing the properties of an isosceles trapezium:

An **isosceles trapezium** is a trapezium in which the two opposite non-parallel sides are the same length.	True ☐	False ☐
Its diagonals **bisect** each other.	True ☐	False ☐
Its diagonals cross at right angles.	True ☐	False ☐
Its diagonals are the same length.	True ☐	False ☐
It has one line of symmetry.	True ☐	False ☐
It has a rotational symmetry of order 2.	True ☐	False ☐

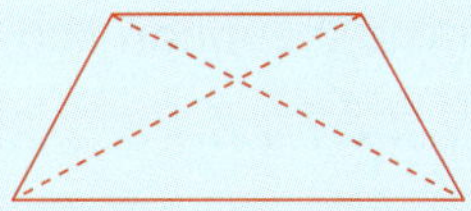

Practice

1 Each of these shapes is made from two polygons. Draw lines to show the join. One has been done for you.

a) Isosceles trapezium and rhombus

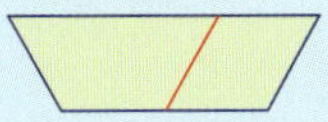

b) Square and kite

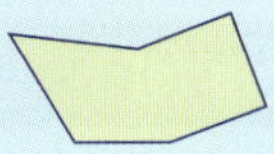

c) Trapezium and kite

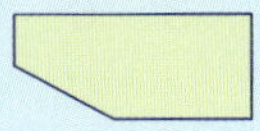

d) Trapezium and parallelogram

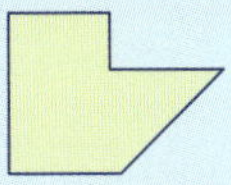

e) Trapezium and triangle

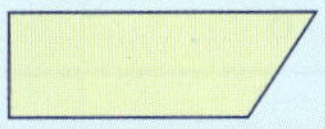

f) Rhombus and an arrowhead

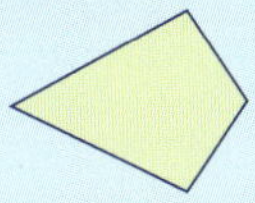

g) Irregular quadrilateral and parallelogram

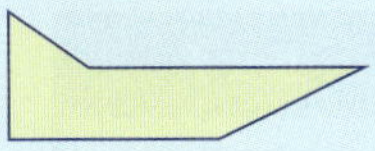

h) Rectangle and hexagon

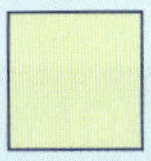

i) Trapezium and trapezium

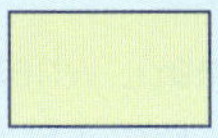

How did I do?

	✔
I know what congruent means.	☐
I can recognise congruent shapes.	☐
I can recognise and describe properties of 2-D shapes.	☐

22: Statistics

In this unit you will revise:
- the mode, median, mean and range
- how to find the mean of a set of data in a table
- how to calculate the mean using an assumed mean.

When you are reorganising a set of data, always cross off the numbers as you count them and always check that you have the correct total at the end.

What you should know

Statistics means collecting, organising and analysing data. One way of analysing data is to find averages. **Averages** are used to represent a middle or typical value in a set of numbers. There are three types of average: **mean**, **median** and **mode**. The mode, median and mean of a set of numbers can be found, like this:

Rob's Maths test scores (out of 10): 4 3 7 8 3

- to find the **mode** look for the most popular, or frequent, value or values in the list.

  4, 3, 7, 8, 3 most frequent value the **mode** is **3**

- to find the **median** put all the scores in order and then find the middle value. If there are two middle values then the median is the number half-way between them.

  3, 3, 4, 7, 8 middle value the **median** is **4**

- to find the **mean** find the total of all the scores and then divide this by the number of scores.

  $4 + 3 + 7 + 8 + 3 = 25$ $25 \div 5 = 5$ the **mean** is **5**

The **range** is the difference between the highest and lowest values. It also helps to give us a sense of how sets of data differ. The range here is 5, which is found by subtracting 3 from 8.

Get started

Sometimes data is presented in a **frequency** table, which can make it more difficult to find averages.

The same set of scores is shown here in two ways:

4 7 7 5 5 6 6 7 7

Scores (*s*)	Frequency (*f*)
4	1
5	2
6	2
7	4

To find the **mean**, when the data is in a table, multiply each score by its frequency and add these values. Then divide by the total frequency. It can help to draw an extra column and row in the table.

Scores (*s*)	Frequency (*f*)	$s \times f$
4	1	4
5	2	10
6	2	12
7	4	28
Totals	9	54

$54 \div 9 = 6$ the **mean** is **6**

1 Find the mean of this set of data, by completing the table:

Scores (s)	Frequency (f)	$s \times f$
2	1	
3	2	
4	7	
5	6	
6	4	
Totals		

Mean = _______

To find the mean using a mental method, use an **assumed mean** as explained below.

Find the mean of these numbers: 48.6, 51.2, 52.1, 49.9, 50.2

1. Look at the values and choose an easy number that lies somewhere in the middle. Call this the 'assumed mean':

   50.0

2. Find the differences between each number and the assumed mean, saying whether they are more or less using the positive or negative signs.

   −1.4, +1.2, +2.1, −0.1, +0.2

3. Find the total of all these differences (watch out, this might be negative). +2.0
4. Then divide this number by the number of values. $2.0 \div 5 = 0.4$
5. Finally add this total to your assumed mean. This is the actual mean. <u>50.4</u>

Practice

1 Use an assumed mean to find the mean of each set of numbers:

a) 10.2, 9.9, 10.4, 9.9 mean = _______

b) 10.2, 9.7, 10.1, 9.6 mean = _______

c) 11.9, 12.2, 11.7, 11.4 mean = _______

d) 8.1, 8.3, 8.5, 7.9, 7.7 mean = _______

e) 15.7, 16.3, 16.3, 16.8, 15.9 mean = _______

f) 63.2, 63.8, 63.4, 62.8, 63.8 mean = _______

g) 37.6, 38.5, 38.2, 38.4, 37.3 mean = _______

h) 24.6, 24.3, 25.1, 25.3, 24.7 mean = _______

2 The mean of four numbers is 9.8.

These are three of the numbers: 10.1, 10.2, 9.5, ...

Find the fourth number.

How did I do?

	✔
I know how to find the mean, median, mode and range of data in a list.	☐
I can calculate the mean of a set of data in a table.	☐
I can calculate the mean using an assumed mean.	☐

23: Graphs and charts

In this unit you will revise:

- discrete and continuous data
- bar charts and frequency diagrams
- scatter graphs.

When looking at graphs, always read the numbers on the scale carefully. When finding the height of a bar on a bar chart it can help to draw extra lines across the graph with a ruler.

What you should know

A **pie chart** shows information as different sized portions of a circle. It can help you to compare proportions.

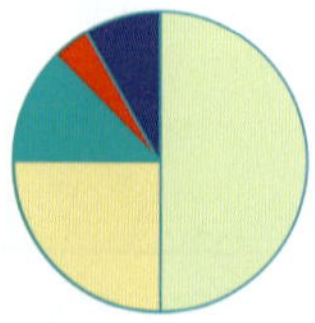

A pie chart

A **bar chart** shows information as vertical or horizontal bars. Often bar charts are used to show frequency and also might show **grouped data**.

A **bar-line graph** shows information as lines. It is similar to a bar chart and often shows frequency.

A **line graph** shows points joined together. It is used commonly for time graphs and for information that has been measured.

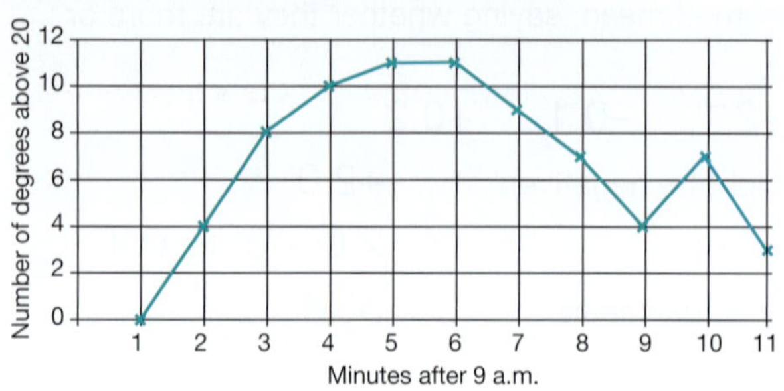

A line graph

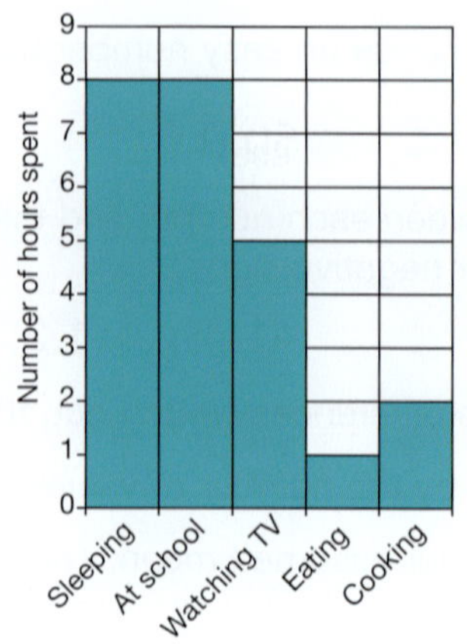

A bar chart

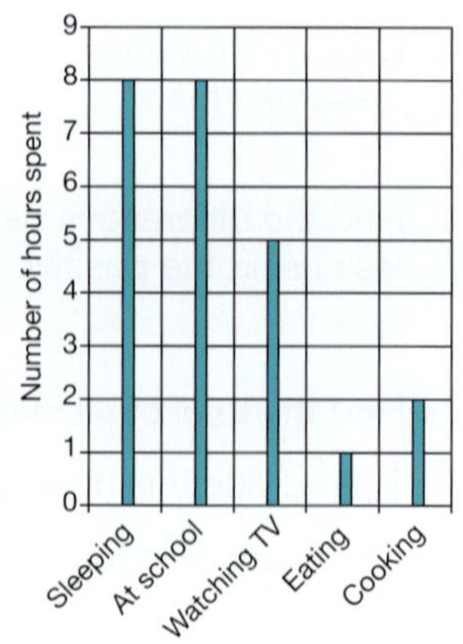

A bar-line graph

Get started

There are two types of data: **discrete data** and **continuous data**.

Discrete data is information about numbers of things that can be counted, like the coins in your pocket or the cars in the car-park.

Continuous data is data collected by measuring things, such as length, mass or time. It is data that, if we used smaller units of measurement, it could be measured more accurately. For discrete data, intermediate values have no meaning, like saying 3.7 cars, whereas, for continuous data, intermediate values, like 3.7 kg, have meaning.

A bar chart with separate bars is usually used to represent discrete data. When continuous data is shown, the bars on the chart always touch each other. In this instance, the chart can be called a **frequency diagram**, like the one shown here:

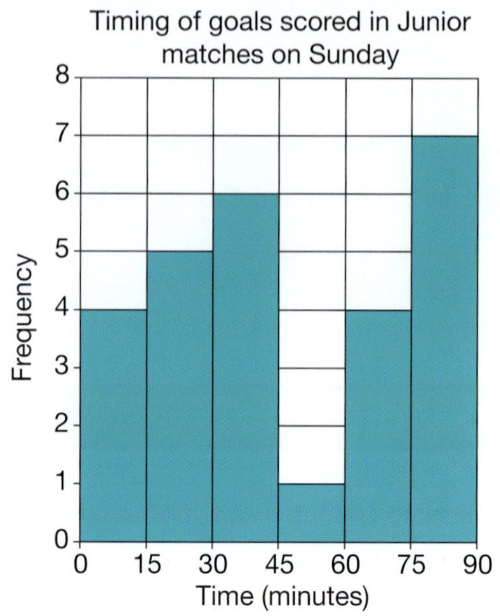

1 Answer these questions about the frequency diagram at the foot of page 50:

a) How many goals were scored in the first fifteen minutes? __________

b) During which time period were 7 goals scored? Between ________ and ________ minutes

c) How many goals were scored in the time period $60 \le t < 75$, where t stands for time? ________

d) A goal was scored in the 45th minute. How many other goals were scored in the time period $45 \le t < 60$? __________

Scatter graphs show whether there is a connection between two sets of values. A graph could show:

- that one value increases as the other increases (positive correlation)
- that one value increases as the other decreases (negative correlation)
- no connection at all (zero correlation).

The arrangement of the dots on the graph shows whether the correlation is positive, negative or zero.

POSITIVE

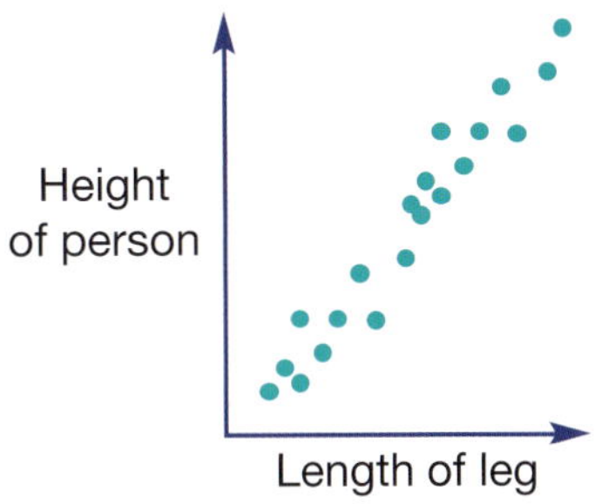

NEGATIVE

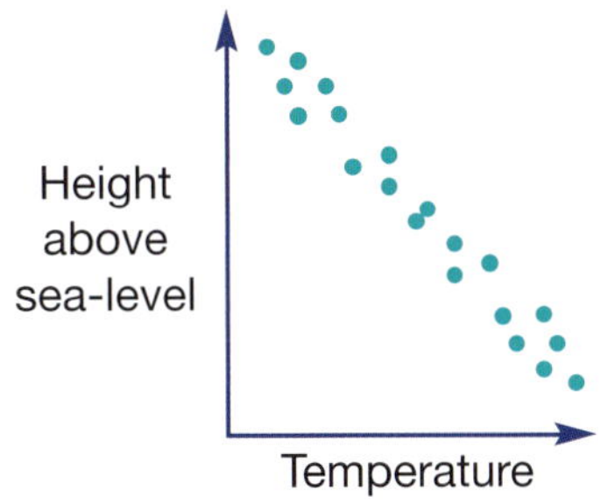

ZERO

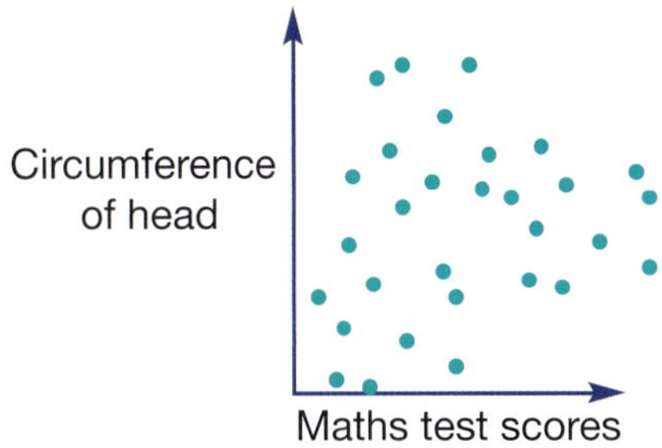

Practice

1 Do you think there is a connection between the two types of data in each pair? Sketch what you think a scatter graph would look like for these data:

a)

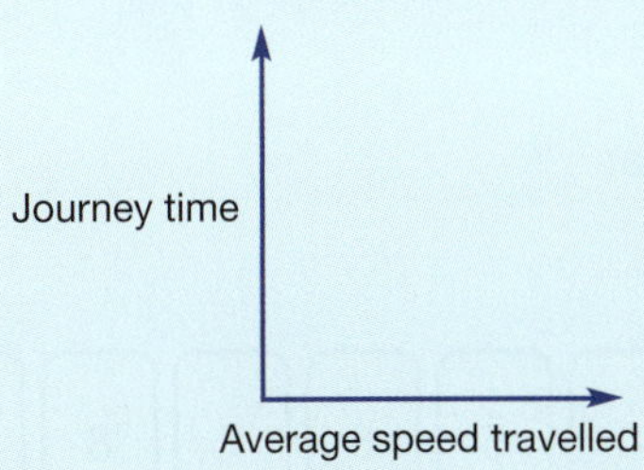

b)

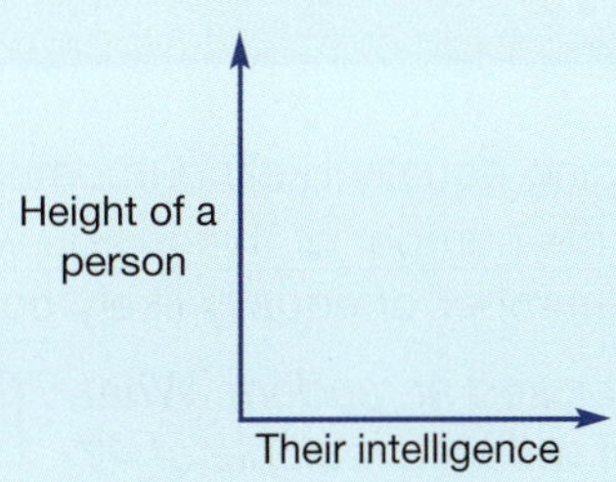

c)

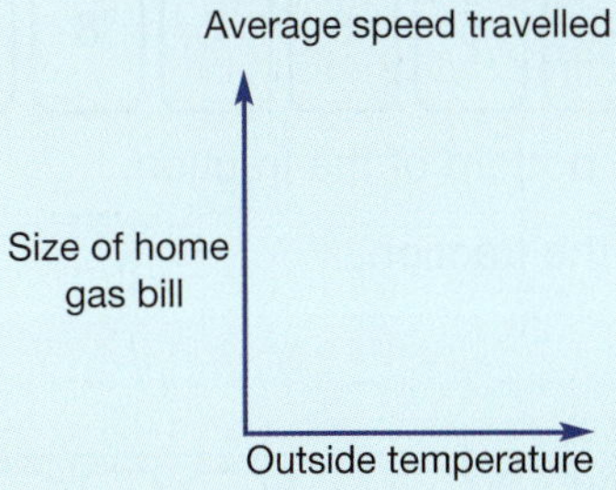

d)

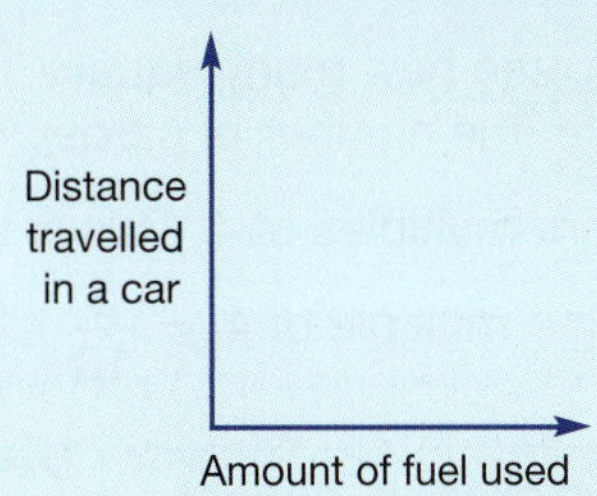

How did I do?

	✔
I know the difference between discrete and continuous data.	☐
I can read and interpret bar charts and frequency diagrams.	☐
I know how scatter graphs show connections between sets of values.	☐

24: Probability

In this unit you will revise:

- how to find probabilities based on equally likely outcomes
- how to find all possible mutually exclusive outcomes using tables.

When a test or exam is getting closer, don't worry about it. Use the checklist at the back of this book. It will help you to realise how much you already know and can point you towards topics that you need to revise a little more.

What you should know

Probability is about the chance, or likelihood, of something happening.

We can measure the probability of something happening in several ways:

1) Seeing how often it has happened before

To find the probability of it snowing on 25 December a person can find out how often it has happened in the past. When this is known an estimate can be made as to the likelihood of a white Christmas. It could be said, in our opinion, it is 'unlikely' or 'very unlikely'.

2) By doing an experiment

To find the probability of throwing a total of 7 with two dice, the dice could be thrown lots of times and the results recorded. The more times the dice are thrown the more accurate the result will be.

The experiment can help you to estimate the likelihood of scoring 7.

3) Using equally likely outcomes

To work out the probability of picking a heart at random from a pack of cards first find out what the possible **outcomes** are. They are heart, diamond, club or spade.

So there are four outcomes and, because there is the same number of cards in each suit, each of these outcomes is **equally likely**. So the probability of picking a heart is 1 out of 4 or $\frac{1}{4}$.

Get started

To find a probability using equally likely outcomes you can use this formula:

$$\text{Probability (P)} = \frac{\text{the number of things you want}}{\text{the number of equally likely outcomes}}$$

One of these cards is picked at random. What is the probability that it will be a multiple of 4?

0	1	2	3	4	5	6	7	8	9

To answer this question, see how many equally likely outcomes there are (the number of cards). This is the number on the bottom of the fraction.

Next count how many are multiples of 4. This is the number on the top of the fraction.

Probability (P) of picking a multiple of 4 $= \frac{2}{10}$

1 One of these cards is picked at random.

1	2	3	4	5	6	7	8	9	10	11	12

What is the probability that it will be:

a) an odd number? _____ **b)** a multiple of 3? _____ **c)** a number greater than 8? _____

d) a 9? _____ **e)** a number greater than 5? _____ **f)** a number less than 1? _____

g) a 13? _____ **h)** a **prime number**? _____ **i)** a factor of 12? _____

Sometimes it can help to draw a table to show all the possible outcomes of an event. These two spinners are spun together. The possible outcomes are listed in the table on the right.

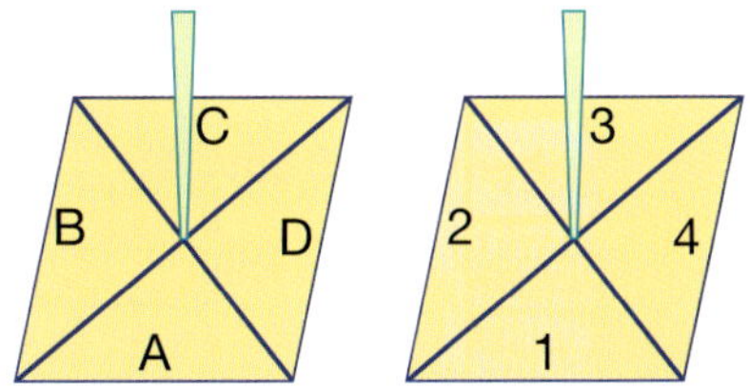

	A	B	C	D
1	A1	B1	C1	D1
2	A2	B2	C2	D2
3	A3	B3	C3	D3
4	A4	B4	C4	D4

This table shows that there are 16 mutually exclusive outcomes. The probability of spinning C3 is $\frac{1}{16}$.

Practice

1 These two spinners are spun together and the **total** is found. List the possible outcomes in the table:

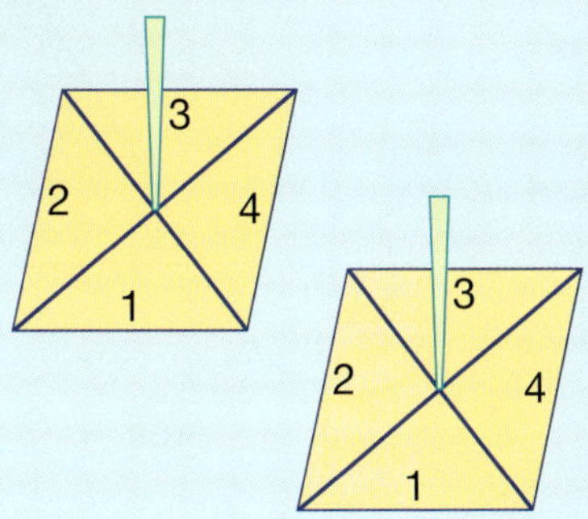

	1	2	3	4
1	2			
2				
3				
4				

What is the probability of:

a) spinning a total of 5? ______

b) spinning an even total? ______

c) not spinning a total of 7? ______

d) spinning a total of 3 or 4? ______

e) spinning a total greater than 4? ______

f) not spinning a total of 6? ______

g) not spinning a total of 2 or 3? ______

h) not spinning a total less than 5? ______

2 Fill in this grid to show all the possible outcomes of rolling two dice and then finding the total.

a) Which total is most likely? ________

What is the probability of rolling a total of:

b) 7? ______ **c)** 12? ______

d) 4? ______ **e)** 8? ______

How did I do?

I can find probabilities based on equally likely outcomes. ☐

I know how to use tables to show possible outcomes. ☐

25: Test 3

1 Find the area of each shape by splitting it into parts.

a)

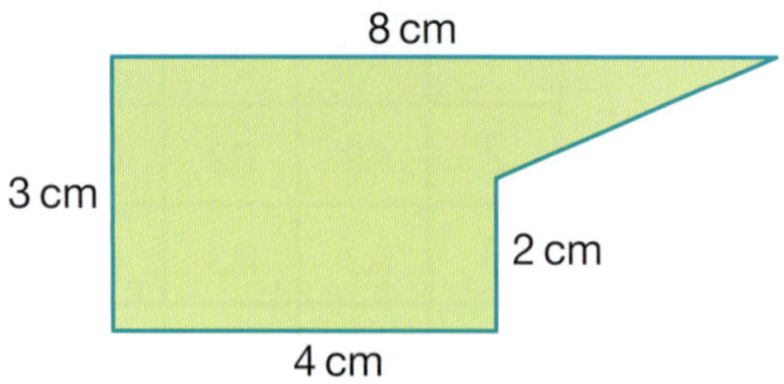

Area = __________ cm^2

b)

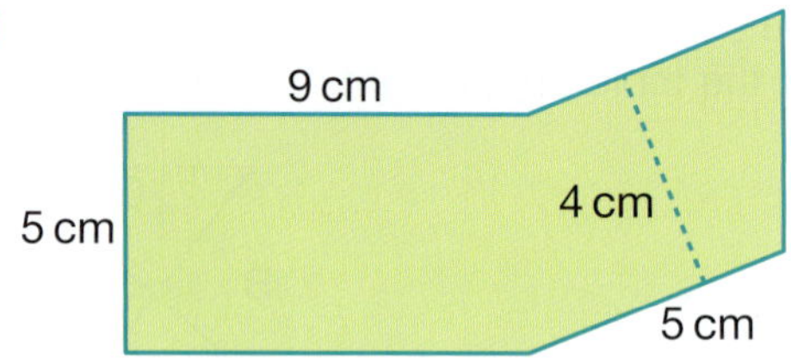

Area = __________ cm^2

c)

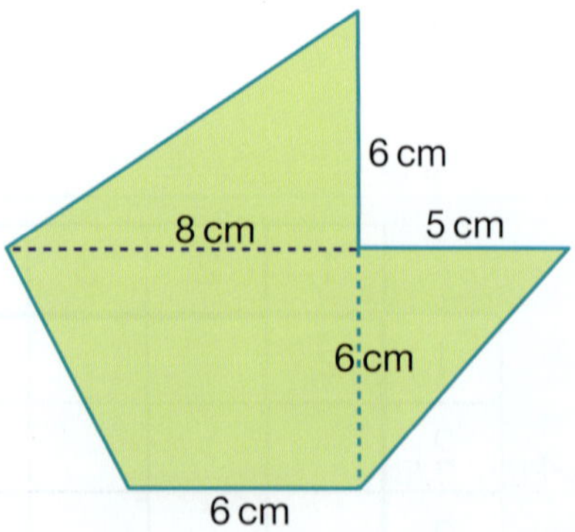

Area = __________ cm^2

d)

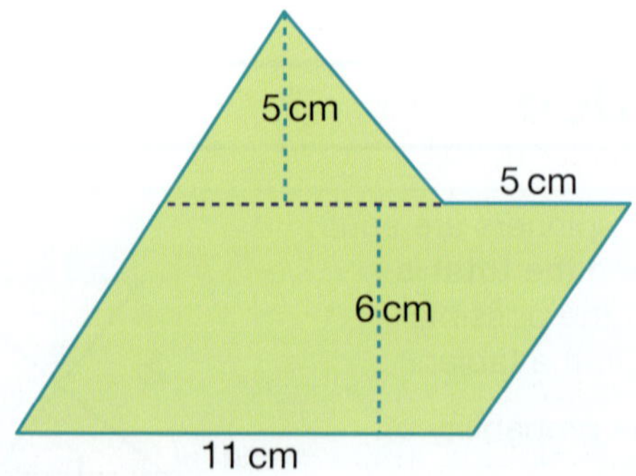

Area = __________ cm^2

2 Construct the **perpendicular bisector** of each of these lines:

3 Construct the **bisector** of each of these angles.

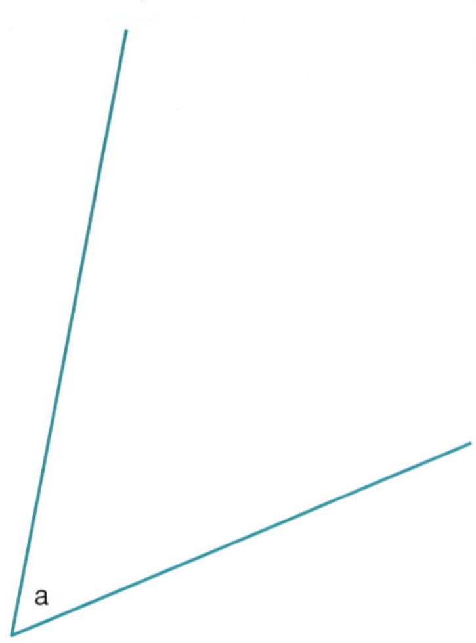

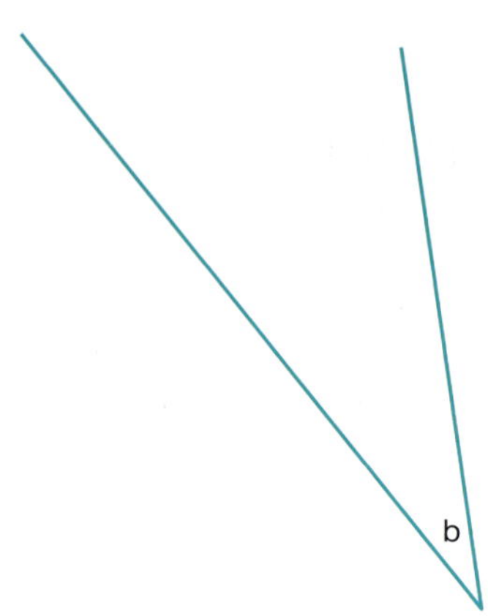

4 Find the co-ordinates of the mid-point (M) of the line PQ if the co-ordinates of P and Q are as follows:

a) P (–6, 2) Q (8, –6) M = (__,__)   b) P (–4, –3) Q (0, 3) M = (__,__)

c) P (6, –9) Q (–4, 5) M = (__,__)   d) P (–3, –5) Q (5, 7) M = (__,__)

e) P (–8, –6) Q (4, 2) M = (__,__)   f) P (–2, 7) Q (8, –1) M = (__,__)

5 Tick whether each sentence is true or false when describing the properties of a parallelogram that is not a rhombus:

A **parallelogram** is a quadrilateral in which both sets of opposite sides are the same length.	True ☐	False ☐
Its diagonals **bisect** each other.	True ☐	False ☐
Its diagonals cross at right angles.	True ☐	False ☐
Its diagonals are the same length.	True ☐	False ☐
It has one line of symmetry.	True ☐	False ☐
It has a rotational symmetry of order 2.	True ☐	False ☐

6 Use an assumed mean to find the mean of each set of numbers:

a) 10.3, 10.0, 10.5, 10.0 mean = ________   b) 10.1, 9.6, 10.0, 9.5 mean = ________

c) 21.9, 22.2, 21.4, 21.7 mean = ________   d) 5.1, 5.3, 5.5, 4.9, 4.7 mean = ________

7 For each of these scatter graphs state whether the correlation is positive, negative or zero.

Number of hours of TV watched each day

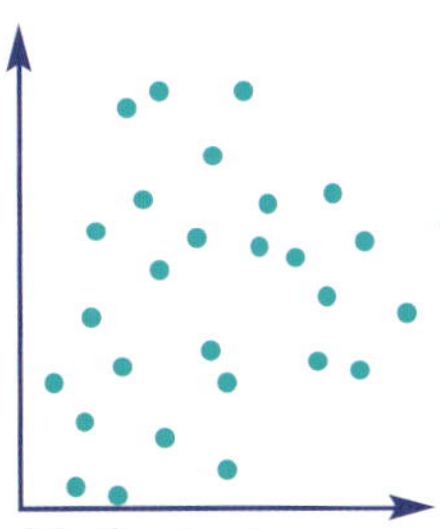

Maths test scores

________ correlation

Size of animal

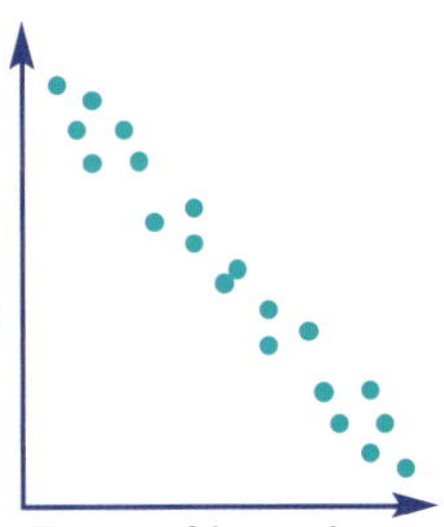

Rate of heartbeat

________ correlation

Number of ice creams sold

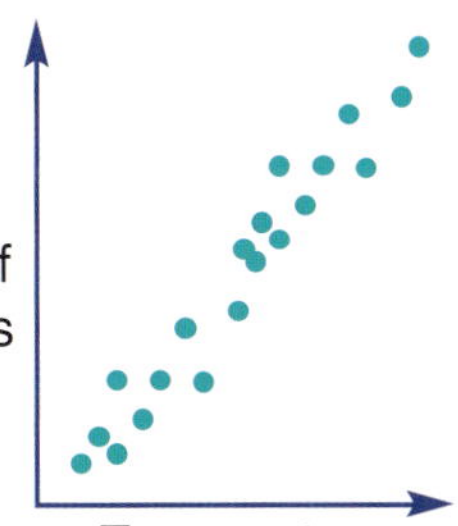

Temperature

________ correlation

8 These two spinners are spun together and the **total** is found.
List the possible outcomes in the table:

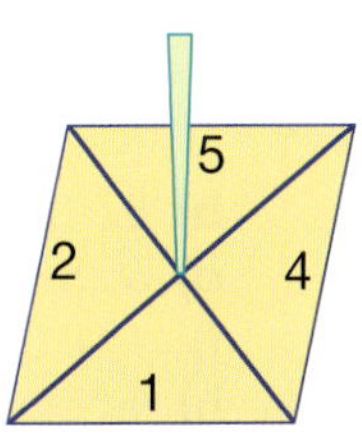

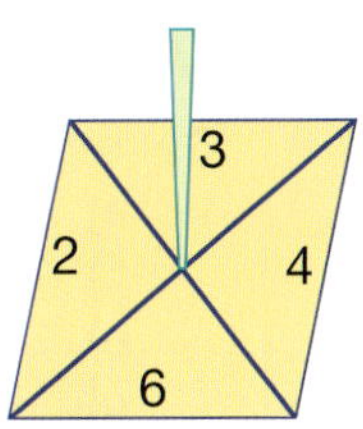

	2	3	4	6
1	3			
2				
4				
5				

What is the probability of:

a) spinning a total of 5? _____   b) spinning an even total? _____

c) not spinning a total of 7? _____   d) spinning a total of 3 or 4? _____

e) spinning a total greater than 4? _____   f) not spinning a total of 6? _____

g) not spinning a total of 3 or 4? _____   h) not spinning a total less than 5? _____

Answers

Unit 1: Pages 6–7

Get started

1 a) One hundred thousand = 10^5
b) One hundred = 10^2
c) One million = 10^6
d) Ten million = 10^7
e) One thousand = 10^3

2 a) 3.4 b) 80.9
c) 0.04 d) 0.008
e) 0.034

3 a) 0.17 b) 28.53
c) 0.013 d) 0.0068
e) 0.0275

Practice

1 a) 10^3 b) 10^5
c) 10^0 d) 10^7
e) 10^1

2 a) 1600 b) 38 400
c) 730 d) 2
e) 1050

3 a) 60 000 b) 780 000
c) 3 520 000 d) 40 700
e) 1200

4 a) 240 b) 4800
c) 350 d) 92
e) 14 f) 2.5
g) 485 h) 36.2

Unit 2: Pages 8–9

Get started

1 Or equivalent fractions:
a) $\frac{16}{24}$✓, $\frac{15}{24}$
b) $\frac{12}{20}$, $\frac{15}{20}$✓
c) $\frac{20}{24}$, $\frac{21}{24}$✓ or $\frac{40}{48}$, $\frac{42}{48}$✓
d) $\frac{70}{90}$, $\frac{72}{90}$✓
e) $\frac{20}{35}$, $\frac{21}{35}$✓

2 $\frac{10}{24}$, $\frac{15}{24}$, $\frac{16}{24}$, $\frac{18}{24}$, $\frac{20}{24}$

3 a) 0.222…, 0.25, 0.3, 0.6, 0.625
b) 0.4, 0.444…, 0.667, 0.833, 0.875

Practice

1 a) $\frac{5}{20}$, $\frac{6}{20}$, $\frac{7}{20}$, $\frac{8}{20}$
b) $\frac{14}{24}$, $\frac{15}{24}$, $\frac{16}{24}$, $\frac{18}{24}$, $\frac{20}{24}$
c) $\frac{16}{36}$, $\frac{20}{36}$, $\frac{22}{36}$, $\frac{27}{36}$, $\frac{30}{36}$

2 a) 0.6, 0.625, 0.7, 0.75, 0.85
b) 0.48, 0.53, 0.6, 0.67, 0.7
c) 0.1666, 0.25, 0.333, 0.375, 0.417

3 a) 0.2
b) 0.875
c) 0.556

Unit 3: Pages 10–11

Get started

1 a) £12.10 b) 7.2 m
c) £21 d) 63 g
e) 107.1 cm f) 20.8 m
g) 30.4 cm h) 114 kg

2 a) 65% b) 32%
c) 80% d) 60%
e) 28% f) 45%
g) 72% h) 90%

Practice

1 Clockwise from £122.40: £2.40, £26.40, £36, £228, £84, £98.40, £62.40

2 Andy = 80%, Mandy = 84%✓, Sandy = 70%

3 80%

4 68.4%

Unit 4: Pages 12–13

Get started

1 a) D = 0.1, P = 10%
D = 0.75, P = 75%
D = 0.27, P = 27%
b) P = 1%, F = $\frac{1}{100}$
P = 40%, F = $\frac{2}{5}$
P = 81%, F = $\frac{81}{100}$
c) F = $\frac{27}{100}$, D = 0.27
F = $\frac{1}{20}$, D = 0.05
F = $\frac{1}{5}$, D = 0.2

Practice

1 a) $\frac{39}{100}$ b) 8%
c) $\frac{16}{25}$ d) 31%

2 a) $\frac{7}{8}$, 0.875, 87.5% b) $\frac{11}{14}$, 0.786, 78.6%
c) $\frac{2}{3}$, 0.667, 66.7%

3 0.83, 83%, $\frac{83}{100}$

Unit 5: Pages 14–15

Get started

1 a) 2 : 3 b) 5 : 12
c) 4 : 1 d) 3 : 5
e) 1 : 5 f) 1 : 2
g) 3 : 2 h) 1 : 3

2 a) 4 : 1 b) 9 : 100
c) 1 : 15 d) 3 : 4
e) 5 : 4 f) 13 : 10

Practice

1 a) 10 : 1
b) 1 : 8
c) 3 : 5

2 a) Males: 45, Females: 18
b) Ali: £10, Baz: £20, Colin: £50
c) Deepa: £16, Ella: £64, Fee: £80

Unit 6: Pages 16–17

Get started

1 **a)** 3 **b)** 3
c) 4 **d)** 6
e) 4 **f)** –8
g) –4 **h)** –10
i) –5 **j)** –9

2 **a)** 1 + 4 = 5 **b)** –5 + 8 = 3
c) –4 – 7 = –11 **d)** 6 – 4 = 2
e) 8 + 8 =16 **f)** –3 – 3 = –6

Practice

1 **a)** –4 **b)** 4
c) –4 **d)** 10
e) 3 **f)** 15
g) –5 **h)** –4

2 **a)** 10 **b)** –45
c) –3 **d)** 7
e) –40 **f)** 48
g) 9 **h)** –4
i) 10 **j)** –24
k) 3 **l)** –4

3 **a)** –4, –6 or –6, –4 **b)** –3, –6
c) –4, 6 or 6, –4 **d)** –18, –6

Unit 7: Pages 18–19

Get started

1 **a)** [12: 1, 2, 3, 4, 6, 12; 24: 1, 2, 3, 4, 6, 8, 12, 24] CF: 1, 2, 3, 4, 6, 12
b) [45: 1, 3, 5, 9, 15, 45; 27: 1, 3, 9, 27] CF: 1, 3, 9
c) [28: 1, 2, 4, 7, 14, 28; 32: 1, 2, 4, 8, 16, 32] CF: 1, 2, 4
d) [18: 1, 2, 3, 6, 9, 18; 30: 1, 2, 3, 5, 6, 10, 15, 30] CF: 1, 2, 3, 6
e) [24: 1, 2, 3, 4, 6, 8, 12, 24; 40: 1, 2, 4, 5, 8, 10, 20, 40] CF: 1, 2, 4, 8
f) [30: 1, 2, 3, 5, 6, 10, 15, 30; 36: 1, 2, 3, 4, 6, 9, 12, 18, 36] CF: 1, 2, 3, 6

2 **a)** 12 **b)** 9
c) 4 **d)** 6
e) 8 **f)** 6

3 **a)** 15, 30, 45 **b)** 12, 24, 36
c) 28, 56, 84 **d)** 9, 18, 27
e) 35, 70, 105 **f)** 24, 48, 72

4 **a)** 15 **b)** 12
c) 28 **d)** 9
e) 35 **f)** 24

Practice

1 **a)** 72, 80 **b)** 72, 42 or 54, 42
c) 42, 35 **d)** 80, 35
e) 80, 42 or 54, 80 **f)** 72, 54

2 **a)** 66 **b)** 40
c) 12 **d)** 60
e) 60

Unit 8: Pages 20–21

Get started

1 **a)** 49 **b)** ±5
c) 81 **d)** ±7
e) 100 **f)** 25
g) ±2 **h)** 36
i) ±3 **j)** 144

2 **a)** 125 **b)** 4
c) 2 **d)** 1000
e) 1

Practice

1 **a)** 1024 **b)** ±54
c) 2304 **d)** ±92
e) 169 **f)** 343
g) 8 **h)** 6
i) 729 **j)** 1331

2 **a)** ±18 **b)** 2025
c) Correct **d)** 262 144
e) 0.01 **f)** ±268
g) Correct **h)** Correct
i) Correct

3 **a)** 49 **b)** ±4
c) 0 **d)** n^2
e) 6.9

Unit 9: Pages 22–23

Test 1

1 **a)** 10^4 **b)** 10^6
c) 10^1 **d)** 10^8
e) 10^0

2 **a)** 2400 **b)** 64 300
c) 690 **d)** 4
e) 3060

3 **a)** 70 000 **b)** 440 000
c) 2 620 000 **d)** 50 300
e) 1600

4 **a)** 370 **b)** 4700
c) 280 **d)** 69
e) 27 **f)** 2.9
g) 155 **h)** 42.7

5 **a)** $\frac{9}{20}, \frac{12}{20}, \frac{14}{20}, \frac{15}{20}$
b) $\frac{9}{24}, \frac{10}{24}, \frac{16}{24}, \frac{16}{24}$

6 **a)** 0.48, $\frac{2}{3}$, $\frac{7}{10}$, 0.75, $\frac{11}{12}$
b) 0.25, 0.3333, $\frac{3}{8}$, $\frac{9}{12}$, $\frac{5}{6}$

7 Andy = 70%, Mandy = 76%✓, Sandy = 65%

8 **a)** D = 0.7, P = 70%
D = 0.4, P = 40%
D = 0.63, P = 63%
b) P = 7%, F = $\frac{7}{100}$
P = 30%, F = $\frac{3}{10}$
P = 17%, F = $\frac{17}{100}$
c) F = $\frac{33}{100}$, D = 0.33
F = $\frac{1}{50}$, D = 0.02
F = $\frac{2}{5}$, D = 0.4

9 **a)** $\frac{7}{12}$, 0.583, 58.3%
b) $\frac{1}{2}$, 0.5, 50%
c) $\frac{5}{8}$, 0.625, 62.5%

10 **a)** 10 : 1
b) 1 : 10
c) 3 : 10

11 **a)** Males: 25, Females: 10
b) Ali: £160, Baz: £240, Colin: £400
c) Deepa: £4, Ella: £16, Fee: £28

12 **a)** −9 **b)** 6
c) −8 **d)** 5
e) −5 **f)** 12
g) −12 **h)** 1

13 **a)** 8 **b)** −36
c) −10 **d)** 9
e) −60 **f)** 32
g) 7 **h)** −8
i) 12 **j)** −27
k) 6 **l)** −8

14 **a)** 10 **b)** 4
c) 12 **d)** 7
e) 6

15 **a)** 77 **b)** 8
c) 12 **d)** 24
e) 30

16 **a)** 729 **b)** ±15
c) 1225 **d)** ±21
e) 121 **f)** 216
g) 10 **h)** 14
i) 512 **j)** 13 824

Unit 10: Pages 24–25

Get started

1 **a)** 3 **b)** 2
c) 2 **d)** 4
e) 4 **f)** 2
g) 9 **h)** 0.5

2 **a)** 32 **b)** 48
c) 78 **d)** 1
e) 1 **f)** 8
g) 26 **h)** 38
i) 5

Practice

1 **a)** 10 **b)** 2
c) 0.5 **d)** 5
e) 1 **f)** 1.5

2 All the expressions have the value of 12

3 b, d and f are equal to 100

Unit 11: Pages 26–27

Get started

1 **a)** 35.4 × 2.8 is approx 35 × 3 = 105

354
× 28
2832
7080 Ans must be 99.12 from
9912 approximation above

b) 2.6 × 36.7 is approx 3 × 36 = 108

367
× 26
2202
7340 Ans must be 95.42 from
9542 approximation above

c) 2.85 × 7.4 is approx 3 × 7 = 21

285
× 74
1140
19950 Ans must be 21.09 from
21090 approximation above

d) 9.37 × 5.9 is approx 9 × 6 = 54

937
× 59
8433
46850 Ans must be 55.283 from
55283 approximation above

e) 85.6 ÷ 4 is approx 86 ÷ 4 = 21.5

856
÷ 4 Ans must be 21.4 from
214 approximation above

f) 109.6 ÷ 8 is approx 110 ÷ 8 = 13.75

1096
÷ 8 Ans must be 13.7 from
137 approximation above

g) 239.22 ÷ 6 is approx 240 ÷ 6 = 40

23922
÷ 6 Ans must be 39.87 from
3987 approximation above

h) 2.94 ÷ 7 is approx 3 ÷ 6 = 0.5

294
÷ 7 Ans must be 0.42 from
42 approximation above

Practice

1 10 chairs along each side, so 20 in total

2 8 chairs in each row because 8 × 75 cm = 6 m

3 68

4 **a)** 126 **b)** 88 cm

Unit 12: Pages 28–29

Get started

1 a) $4g + 3h$ b) $6m + n$
c) $x + 3y$ d) $5e + f$
e) $3c + 2d$ f) $5j + 2k$
g) q h) $4s - t$
i) $a - b$

Practice

1 a) $a - b + 4c$ b) $2p + 3q + 3r$
c) $4g - h + 5$ d) $3m + 4n - 3$
e) $c + 2$ f) $3s + t - 3$
g) $w + 6v + 3$ h) $10x - 2y + 4$
i) $7a - 2b - c + 9$

2 $9n + 10m + 11$
$5n + 7m + 1$ $4n + 3m + 10$
$3n + 5m - 4$ $2n + 2m + 5$ $m + 2n + 5$

3 a) $7a + 6$
b) $3e + 1$
c) $15g + 23$

Unit 13: Pages 30–31

Get started

1 a) $a = 8$ b) $y = 3$
c) $f = 4$ d) $p = 3$
e) $d = 10$ f) $c = 8$
g) $b = 8$ h) $e = 4$

2 a) $f = 3$ b) $b = 5$
c) $d = 2.5$ d) $a = 5$
e) $e = 2.5$ f) $c = 5$
g) $g = 7$ h) $h = 3.5$
i) $j = 3$

Practice

1 a) $r = 4$ b) $t = 2$
c) $u = 2$ d) $m = 1$
e) $k = 3$ f) $n = 6$

2 a) $x = 3$, length = 8
b) $y = 18$, length = 60
c) $z = 2$, length = 6

Unit 14: Pages 32–33

Get started

1 a) 40 b) 2
c) 1 d) 100
e) 64 f) 46
g) 30 h) 14
i) 2

2 a) $E = 12$ b) $E = 9$
c) $E = 8$ d) $E = 18$
e) $E = 6$ f) $E = 10$

Practice

1 a)

19	51	−8
38	−32	24
5	11	14

b)

5	51	−15
24	−32	45
12	18	7

c)

57	156	−24
111	−102	72
21	27	33

2 a) 280 cm
b) 118 cm
c) 142 cm
d) 528 cm

Unit 15: Pages 34–35

Get started

1 a) 7, 11, 15, 19, 23
b) −2, 1, 4, 7, 10
c) 15, 10, 5, 0, −5

2 a) nth = $5n$, 10th = 50
b) nth = $4n$, 10th = 40

Practice

1 a) 2, 4, 6, 8, 10, 12
b) nth term = $2n$
c) 10th term = 20 squares

2 a) 6, 11, 16, 21, 26
b) 4, 6, 8, 10, 12
c) 9, 8, 7, 6, 5

Unit 16: Pages 36–37

Get started

1 a) 5, 3, 1, −1, −3
(−2, 5), (−1, 3), (0, 1), (1, −1), (2, −3)

b)

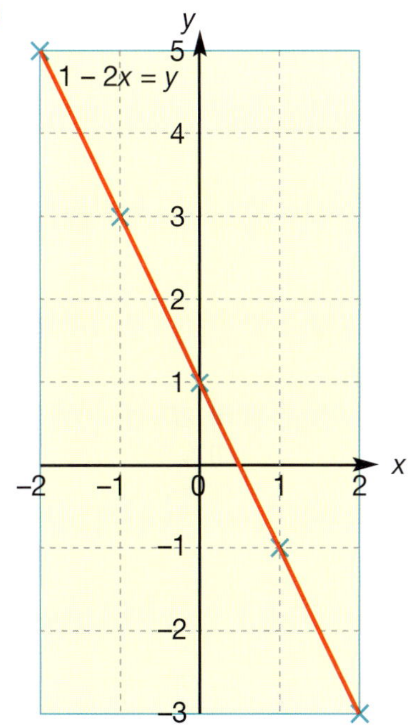

Practice

1 a) Grad = 3, Int = −1
b) Grad = −2, Int = 4
c) Grad = 8, Int = 0
d) Grad = 1, Int = −2

Unit 17: Pages 38–39

Test 2

1 **a)** 80 **b)** 64
c) 30 **d)** 1
e) 1 **f)** 16
g) 35 **h)** 30
i) 3

2 **a)** 0.5 **b)** 4
c) 4 **d)** 7

3 **a)** 65.28 **b)** 159.84
c) 19.656 **d)** 27.927
e) 21.4 **f)** 13.7
g) 39.87 **h)** 0.42

4 22

5 $7n + 8m + 15$
$3n + 5m + 3$ $4n + 3m + 12$
$2n + 4m - 3$ $n + m + 6$ $2m + 3n + 6$

6 **a)** $6a + 9$ **b)** $5e + 5$
c) $10g + 23$

7 **a)** $a = 12$ **b)** $y = 10$
c) $f = 1$ **d)** $p = 5$
e) $d = 7$ **f)** $c = 4$
g) $b = 10$ **h)** $e = 4$

8 **a)** $r = 0$ **b)** $t = -2$
c) $u = -15$ **d)** $m = -5$
e) $k = 4$ **f)** $n = 1$

9 131 300 −35
233 −198 105
32 38 70

10 **a)** 7, 13, 19, 25, 31
b) 2, 6, 10, 14, 18
c) 7, 6, 5, 4, 3

11 **a)** Grad = 2, Int = −1
b) Grad = −3, Int = 5
c) Grad = 5, Int = 0
d) Grad = 1, Int = −4

Unit 18: Pages 40–41

Get started

1 **a)** 30 cm^2 **b)** 20 cm^2
c) 35 cm^2 **d)** 6 cm^2
e) 28 cm^2 **f)** 9 cm^2

2 **a)** 28 cm^2 **b)** 45 cm^2
c) 36 cm^2 **d)** 24 cm^2
e) 24 cm^2 **f)** 45.5 cm^2

Practice

1 **a)**111 cm^2 **b)** 96 cm^2
c) 57.5 cm^2 **d)** 62 cm^2

Unit 19: Pages 42–43

Get started

1 Check perpendicular bisectors are at 90° to original lines
2 Check two halves of original angles are equal

Practice

1 Check your constructions
2 Check your constructions

Unit 20: Pages 44–45

Get started

1 **a)** A = (−1, 4), B = (5, 4),
mid-point: (2, 4)
b) C = (−4, 3), D = (4, 3),
mid-point = (0, 3)
c) E = (−6, 5), F = (−6, −3),
mid-point = (−6, 1)
d) C = (−4, 3), E = (−6, 5),
mid-point = (−5, 4)
e) B = (5, 4), H = (1, 0),
mid-point = (3, 2)
f) F = (−6, −3), G = (−3, 0),
mid-point = (−4.5, −1.5)

2 **a)** (1, 1) **b)** (−1, −3)
c) (0, −2) **d)** (−3, 1)

Practice

1 **a)** (1, −2) **b)** (1, 0)
c) (1, −2) **d)** (−4, 1)
e) (−2, −1) **f)** (3, 2)
g) (4, −5) **h)** (1, −5)
i) (−0.5, −1) **j)** (−0.5, −3)

Unit 21: Pages 46–47

Get started

1 **a)** The third, fourth and seventh shapes from left to right
b) The second, fourth and seventh shapes
c) The first, second and sixth shapes
d) The second, third, fifth and sixth shapes

2 True
False
True
False
True
False
False

3 True
False
False
True
True
False

Practice

1 a) 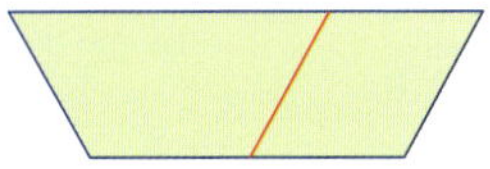

b) 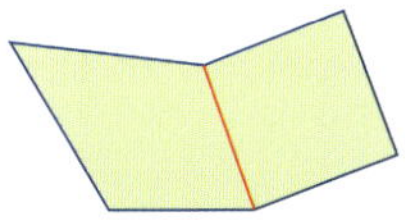

c) 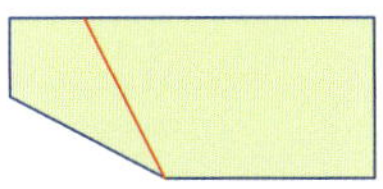

d) 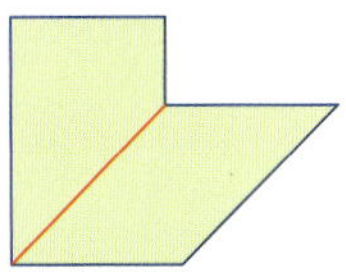

e) 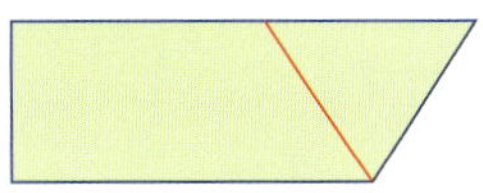

f) 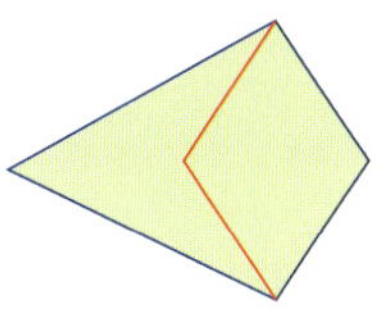

g) 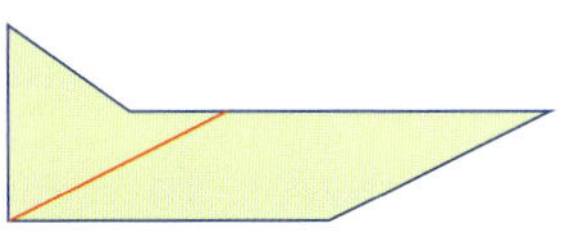

h) 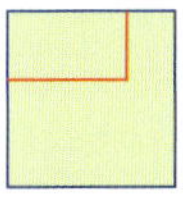

i) 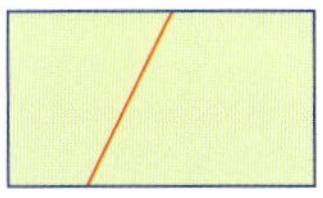

Unit 22: Pages 48–49

Get started

1 Mean = 4.5

Practice

1 **a)** 10.1 **b)** 9.9
c) 11.8 **d)** 8.1
e) 16.2 **f)** 63.4
g) 38 **h)** 24.8

2 9.4

Unit 23: Pages 50–51

Get started

1 **a)** 4 **b)** 75 and 90
c) 4 **d)** 0

Practice

1 **a)** Negative correlation
b) Zero correlation
c) Negative correlation
d) Positive correlation

Unit 24: Pages 52–53

Get started

1 **a)** $\frac{6}{12}$ or $\frac{1}{2}$ **b)** $\frac{4}{12}$ or $\frac{1}{3}$
c) $\frac{4}{12}$ or $\frac{1}{3}$ **d)** $\frac{1}{12}$
e) $\frac{7}{12}$ **f)** 0
g) 0 **h)** $\frac{5}{12}$
i) $\frac{6}{12}$ or $\frac{1}{2}$

Practice

1 **a)** $\frac{1}{4}$ **b)** $\frac{1}{2}$
c) $\frac{7}{8}$ **d)** $\frac{5}{16}$
e) $\frac{5}{8}$ **f)** $\frac{13}{16}$
g) $\frac{13}{16}$ **h)** $\frac{5}{8}$

2 **a)** 7 **b)** $\frac{1}{6}$
c) $\frac{1}{36}$ **d)** $\frac{1}{12}$
e) $\frac{5}{36}$

Unit 25: Pages 54–55

TEST 3

1 **a)** 14 cm^2 **b)** 65 cm^2
c) 81 cm^2 **d)** 81 cm^2

2 Check perpendicular bisector is at 90° to original line

3 Check two halves of original angle are equal

4 **a)** (1, –2) **b)** (–2, 0)
c) (1, –2) **d)** (1, 1)
e) (–2, –2) **f)** (3, 3)

5 True
True
False
False
False
True

6 **a)** 10.2
b) 9.8
c) 21.8
d) 5.1

7 Zero
Negative
Positive

8 **a)** $\frac{1}{8}$ **b)** $\frac{1}{2}$
c) $\frac{13}{16}$ **d)** $\frac{3}{16}$
e) $\frac{13}{16}$ **f)** $\frac{7}{8}$
g) $\frac{13}{16}$ **h)** $\frac{13}{16}$

Checklist

Tick off each topic when you feel confident that you understand it.

Place value ✔

- powers of 10 ☐
- how to multiply integers and decimals by 0.1 and 0.01 ☐
- how to divide integers and decimals by 0.1 and 0.01 ☐

Fractions

- how to order fractions by writing them with a common denominator ☐
- how to use division to convert a fraction to a decimal ☐
- how to order fractions by converting them to decimals ☐

Percentages

- how to calculate percentages of numbers and quantities mentally ☐
- how to write one number as a percentage of another without a calculator ☐
- how to write one number as a percentage of another with a calculator ☐

Proportion

- the equivalence of percentages, fractions and decimals ☐
- how to use fractions, decimals and percentages to compare proportions ☐

Ratio

- how to reduce a ratio to its simplest form ☐
- how to reduce a ratio in different units to its simplest form ☐
- how to divide a quantity into two or more parts in a given ratio ☐

Integers

- adding and subtracting integers ☐
- multiplying and dividing integers ☐

Factors and multiples

- what factors and multiples are and how to find factors and multiples of numbers ☐
- how to find common factors and to find the highest common factor ☐
- how to find common multiples and to find the lowest common multiple ☐

Powers and roots

- squares and cubes including how to write them using powers ☐
- square roots and cube roots ☐

Calculation strategies

- adding, subtracting, multiplying and dividing using mental methods ☐
- the order of operations, including brackets ☐

Calculations and problems

- adding, subtracting, multiplying and dividing decimals using written methods ☐
- how to check a result by working backwards ☐
- how to solve word problems ☐

Simplifying expressions

- how to simplify or transform an expression by collecting like terms ☐
- how to collect like terms including those in subtractions ☐

Equations

- solving equations with an unknown on either side ☐
- solving equations with unknowns on both sides ☐

Formulae and substituting

- that algebraic operations follow the same order as arithmetic operations ☐
- how to substitute integers into expressions involving small powers ☐
- how to substitute integers into simple formulae and to find unknown values ☐

Sequences

- how to describe sequences using term-to-term and position-to-term rules ☐
- how to generate sequences using position-to-term rules ☐
- describing the nth term of a sequence ☐

Straight line graphs

- how to plot straight line graphs, where y is given explicitly in terms of x ☐
- how equations of the form $y = mx + c$ correspond to straight line graphs ☐

Area

- the formulae for the area of a triangle, parallelogram and trapezium ☐
- how to calculate areas of compound shapes ☐

Construction

- how to construct the perpendicular bisector of a line ☐
- how to construct a bisector of an angle ☐

Co-ordinates

- plotting co-ordinates in all four quadrants ☐
- how to find the co-ordinates of a mid-point along a line ☐

2-D shapes

- what congruent means ☐
- how to recognise congruent shapes ☐
- the names and properties of 2-D shapes ☐

Statistics

- the mode, median, mean and range ☐
- how to find the mean of a set of data in a table ☐
- how to calculate the mean using an assumed mean ☐

Graphs and charts

- discrete and continuous data ☐
- bar charts and frequency diagrams ☐
- scatter graphs ☐

Probability

- how to find probabilities based on equally likely outcomes ☐
- how to find all possible mutually exclusive outcomes using tables ☐

Glossary

Ascending sequences are those where the **terms** in the sequence get larger.

BODMAS – a way of helping you to remember the order to calculate.

Continuous data is data collected by measuring things. It is data that, if we used smaller units of measurement, it could be measured more accurately.

The **decimal point** is the dot separating the whole numbers from the part numbers in a decimal.

Descending sequences are those where the **terms** in the sequence get smaller.

Discrete data is information about numbers of things that can be counted, like the coins in your pocket or the cars in the car-park.

Equally likely outcomes means that the possible outcomes of an event are all equally likely to happen. For example, when a dice is rolled there are six equally likely outcomes.

Equations are number sentences that have an equals sign, like $y + 3 = 6$.

Equivalent fractions are fractions with the same value even though they have different numerators (top numbers) and denominators (bottom numbers).

Expressions do not have an equals sign, like $y + 3$.

Factors are whole numbers that divide exactly into another number without a remainder.

The **frequency** of an event is the number of times it happens: for example, the frequency of tossing a coin and getting heads might be 5 out of 10.

Grouped data is data that has been grouped together to make it easier to understand.

Mean is a type of average. To find the mean find the total of all the values and then divide this by the number of values.

Median is a type of average. To find the median put all the values in order and then find the middle value.

Mode is a type of average. To find the mode look for the most popular, or frequent, value in the list.

A **multiple** of a number is any number into which it will divide exactly, without a remainder.

Negative numbers are numbers less than zero, like –4, –6.4, –8.333 and –19.

The **origin** on a graph or co-ordinate grid is the point **(0, 0)**.

An **outcome** is the result of something happening. Whether it will rain or not today has two possible outcomes and picking a day of the week at random has seven outcomes.

Parallel lines are the same distance apart along their whole length. No matter how long the lines are they will never meet. They can be straight or curved.

A **percentage** is a fraction with a denominator of 100, but written in a different way, using the sign %.

Per cent means 'out of every hundred' or 'for every hundred'.

Perpendicular lines are at right angles to each other.

Positive numbers are the numbers normally used all the time, like 4, 27 and 169. They can be written with a plus sign in front like this +4, +27, +169, but normally are not.

Prime numbers are whole numbers that have only two factors, the number itself and 1, e.g. 2, 5, 11, 31.

Probability is about the chance, or likelihood, of something happening.

Proportion is the relationship between part of something and the whole thing. It compares 'part with whole'.

Range is the difference between the highest and lowest values. Find the range by subtracting the smallest from the largest value.

Ratio is the relationship between two or more numbers or quantities. It compares 'part with part'.

Sequences are numbers arranged in a special order. Each number in a sequence is called a **term**.

Simplifying letters means collecting together those that are the same. This is sometimes called **collecting like terms**.

Square numbers are any numbers that have been made by multiplying a number with itself once. 1, 4, 9, 16, 25, 36, 49, 64, 81, 100 are all square numbers.

The **square root** gives us the number that has been multiplied by itself to give a square number.

The **surface area** is the area of all the faces of a 3-D shape added together.

The '***x* axis**' is the horizontal line on a graph and the '***y* axis**' is the vertical one. The plural of **axis** is **axes**.